Recipes & Stories from
the Eternal City

I HEART
ROME

MARIA
PASQUALE

PHOTOGRAPHY BY

ANDREA FEDERICI
AND GIORGIA NOFRINI

Smith
Street
Books

To Rome, my adopted and forever eternal city.
You have been so very good to me,
and my heart is forever yours.

INTRODUCTION

My love affair with Italy started over 20 years ago.

Like all love affairs, it has been exhilarating, exciting and passionate. There have been ups and downs, and times we even almost called it quits.

I was born to Italian parents in Melbourne, but I somehow knew Italy was my destiny. I grew up in a house that was full of people, with regular gatherings centred around cooking and food.

Everything I learnt about food as a child and young adult, I owe to my Italian mother. She arrived in Australia when she was only three years old, and her formative years were spent in a household of Italian migrants trying to make sense of their new life in Australia. She still talks about how a stool was custom-made for her to reach the table and sink. She used to help her mother make pasta at home on a long wooden board, as well as traditional sweets and pastries that eventually became the scents and tastes of my very own childhood.

My father arrived in Australia as a young adult. To this day, after nearly 50 years in his adopted home, Melbourne, he still has an Italian accent, is an Italian soccer fanatic who wakes up during the night to catch matches live from Italy, and is beyond happy when my mum cooks a dish that nostalgically takes him back to his childhood in Abruzzo. Together, my parents instilled in my siblings and me a love for Italy that will live on for generations.

The Italian language was always heard at home, as was Italian music and television. Italian traditions and customs weren't seen as chores or obligations, but simply a way of life. As children, we were encouraged to learn Italian at school, and my brother and I both attended Italian Saturday school. At the time, I remember resenting the fact that other kids got to go out and play on the weekend but I, as a migrant child in Australia, had to sit and perfect my Italian.

Looking back now, I thank them for that decision — because only as an adult can I appreciate that it is a gift to be encouraged to embrace your heritage. And the very gift of this beautiful language has been to connect me to my cultural past through the relationships I have been able to form in the present. From the warm banter at my local market to the affectionate welcome at my local *trattoria*, to deeper conversations about culinary traditions with the greats of Italian cooking, the language itself has taught me what it means to be Italian.

The indelible ties I have to Italy have been ingrained in me since I was a child, nurtured as a teen, and have ultimately defined me as an adult.

I was six years old when I first visited Italy. It was the 1980s and my memories of the small towns of Italy in summer are of eating *gelato* at my uncle's bar, meeting my paternal grandparents, and staying out in the town *piazza* until the wee hours of the morning. I vividly remember stolen sips of my grandfather's homemade wine, and the smell of freshly brewed coffee still conjures an image of my grandmother serving *caffè* to every welcome visitor.

We travelled back to Italy as a family in the 1990s, but my third visit as a 16-year-old was, for me, a turning point.

It was winter, and winter in Italy's central Abruzzo means freezing and below-zero temperatures. It was pig hunting season and I recall waking up one morning to the sound of shots being fired, and to later see a pig hanging to drip and dry in my uncle's garage. The wine we drank was made from the grapes in our family vineyard, and much of the food we ate came from the land. It was the first time I had been exposed to nose-to-tail as a concept, and it sparked my curiosity in food and the things that defined Italian culture — the language, the way of life and the people. That trip changed me forever, and I just knew that, one day, I would live in Italy.

It took me almost 20 years to muster the courage. I visited Rome over a dozen times in my twenties. Every time I left the city, I cried. I felt like I belonged in Rome, and the pull eventually became too profound to ignore. I loved the grandeur of her monuments — the ochre gold of the oldest walls I'd ever seen, and the chaos and winding cobblestone streets that had touches of history at every turn; I couldn't believe that a modern-day bustling metropolis could sit in harmony with relics and ruins of the past. I loved meandering the streets and getting completely lost in them. It made me feel alive. It was all of this that made me fall hopelessly in love with the Eternal City and had me wondering: could a love affair last forever? Well, I wanted to find out.

In 2011, I walked away from my life in Australia and moved to Rome. I had never lived outside of Melbourne; in Rome, I knew only one person. I knew it was going to be hard and it was — the fear, the struggle, the initial feelings of loneliness, and even displacement. What I know now is that it was worth it.

When I first moved to Rome, I knew food would continue to play an important role in my life, but I didn't know just how much. In a country famous for its food, Rome boasts a fascinating and unique cuisine that is intrinsically tied to its history. *Cucina Romana* is founded on the principles of *cucina povera*, literally 'poor food', traditionally consumed by the lower classes, and influences from Ancient Rome through to more recent events are reflected in the food culture of the Eternal City today. Given the passionate nature of Romans as a people, it's no wonder dining is taken pretty seriously. From *carbonara* recipes to artichoke-frying techniques, just about everything food-related is up for discussion and causes much debate in Rome and, of late, around the world.

I began writing HeartRome, the blog, without any objective other than to share my new Italian experiences with family and friends back home. Then through some initial social introductions, I started working in a dream job in food tourism. My blog started to slowly gain traction and, before I knew it, blogging, writing, eating and travelling had become my world. Rome, my muse and inspiration, had become my work, my life, my happiness, my love.

As I started to unravel and uncover her secrets, Rome revealed herself to me as a modern-day marvel of a city. This open-air museum has seen centuries of emperors, Popes, movements, triumphs and tragedies. It is a city where the past and present sit side-by-side and interact in a painfully beautiful, yet often complex kind of way. My neighbourhood, Trastevere, is what film-set backdrops are made of. For me it has been a blank canvas that I have begun to colour and design with my own story; my very own *Roman Holiday* that became a reality.

This book is dedicated to the city that has adopted and nurtured me, that gave me a new lease on life. It is a collection of my stories, recipes I've tasted, snippets of what I've learnt, and the amazing people I've met along the way.

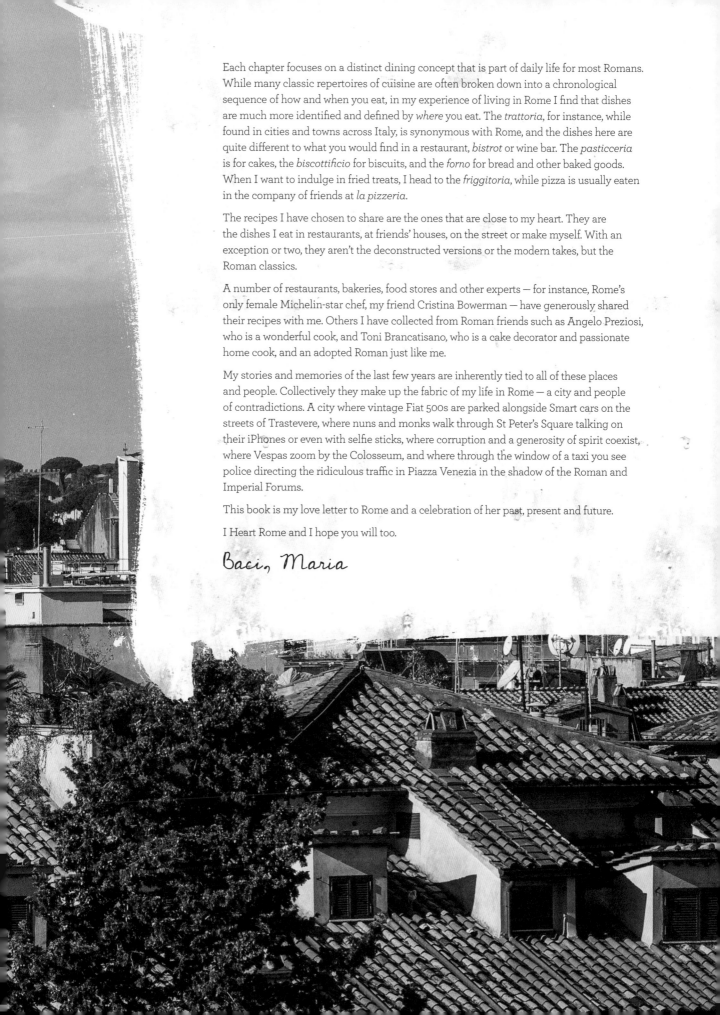

Each chapter focuses on a distinct dining concept that is part of daily life for most Romans. While many classic repertoires of cuisine are often broken down into a chronological sequence of how and when you eat, in my experience of living in Rome I find that dishes are much more identified and defined by *where* you eat. The *trattoria*, for instance, while found in cities and towns across Italy, is synonymous with Rome, and the dishes here are quite different to what you would find in a restaurant, *bistrot* or wine bar. The *pasticceria* is for cakes, the *biscottificio* for biscuits, and the *forno* for bread and other baked goods. When I want to indulge in fried treats, I head to the *friggitoria*, while pizza is usually eaten in the company of friends at *la pizzeria*.

The recipes I have chosen to share are the ones that are close to my heart. They are the dishes I eat in restaurants, at friends' houses, on the street or make myself. With an exception or two, they aren't the deconstructed versions or the modern takes, but the Roman classics.

A number of restaurants, bakeries, food stores and other experts — for instance, Rome's only female Michelin-star chef, my friend Cristina Bowerman — have generously shared their recipes with me. Others I have collected from Roman friends such as Angelo Preziosi, who is a wonderful cook, and Toni Brancatisano, who is a cake decorator and passionate home cook, and an adopted Roman just like me.

My stories and memories of the last few years are inherently tied to all of these places and people. Collectively they make up the fabric of my life in Rome — a city and people of contradictions. A city where vintage Fiat 500s are parked alongside Smart cars on the streets of Trastevere, where nuns and monks walk through St Peter's Square talking on their iPhones or even with selfie sticks, where corruption and a generosity of spirit coexist, where Vespas zoom by the Colosseum, and where through the window of a taxi you see police directing the ridiculous traffic in Piazza Venezia in the shadow of the Roman and Imperial Forums.

This book is my love letter to Rome and a celebration of her past, present and future.

I Heart Rome and I hope you will too.

Baci, Maria

"Rome is not like any other city.
It's a big museum, a living room
that shall be crossed on one's toes."

— ALBERTO SORDI

Chapter One

LA TRAT

TORIA

I will forever cherish my first memories of eating at what has now become my very own *trattoria di fiducia*. The phrase literally means 'my trusted trattoria', but locally it is used in a protective way that indicates, 'This is where I go to eat; this is where they know me.'

Different to a restaurant, the quintessential Roman *trattoria* is where you go for a casual meal with family, colleagues or friends, and where you don't expect fancy food or service. *Trattorie* can be found across the country, but one of the few things Italians can agree on is that Rome embodies *la trattoria Romana* — casual and boisterous, like its people.

In the *trattoria Romana* — where the tablecloths are usually made of paper, and the table turnover is fast — there are no wine glasses, just your average household tumblers, and, in some cases, not even menus. The wait staff will just reel off a list of plates of the day; on Thursdays you'll find gnocchi on most menus, and often on Fridays, more of a focus on fish. And your plate usually hits the table in a pretty abrubt way.

In Rome, even if it's your first time in a *trattoria*, the staff will address you as if they've known you forever. And if you've become a regular at your neighbourhood one, as I have at Da Enzo al 29, my own *trattoria di fiducia*, a visit can be like a homecoming! They know my life story and I theirs, because every time I'm there, we each share a story or two.

The generosity I see in Roman *trattorie* never ceases to amaze me — from offering half-portions of dishes when a patron can't seem to decide what they want to eat, to completely rearranging tables to accommodate families with kids or even a pram.

Especially nowadays, most of the reputable ones in the city use prized produce that is more often than not locally sourced. They may even have a wine list that extends beyond the *vino della casa* (house wine; generally cheap and not created equal — that is, in some *trattorie* it's decent and in others, not so much!).

You go to a *trattoria* in Rome to eat *cucina Romana* — all the traditional Roman dishes that are simple, relatively inexpensive and made to be eaten in good company. This is home to all those dishes that locals and visitors to Rome come to expect. From fried artichokes and stuffed zucchini (courgette) flowers, to lush *primi* (pasta dishes) like the classic Roman quartet of *carbonara*, *cacio e pepe*, *amatriciana* and *la gricia*.

Carbonara, *cacio e pepe* and *amatriciana* have achieved popularity around the world, but *la gricia* is still something of a hidden gem. It's as Roman as it gets, but for some reason never really 'made it' outside of the Eternal City until recently. The first time I ate the dish at a *trattoria* tucked behind Piazza Navona, the waiter described it to me as an 'amatriciana bianca'. *Bianco/a* literally means 'white' in English, but in Italian food terminology it is used to denote a dish that doesn't contain tomatoes or tomato sauce. So, just like the classic *amatriciana*, *la gricia* has crispy *guanciale* (cured pork cheek) and *pecorino* cheese, but no tomato.

As a *secondo* (main course) you might have flame-grilled lamb, *abbacchio allo scottadito* ('scottadito' literally means 'burn your fingers'), *saltimbocca alla Romana* (pan-fried veal with prosciutto and sage), or the more hearty *pollo alla Romana* (roast chicken with peppers).

Dolci (desserts) are often *fatti in casa* (homemade) and range from the classic *tiramisù* to *pannacotta* or the extremely popular tarts. I've included a recipe for my favourite dessert in the city — a delectable, creamy mousse of mascarpone cheese and wild strawberries at Da Enzo.

Dining establishments and trends come and go in Rome, but every Roman has their one neighbourhood *trattoria* that is their go-to, for the warm and uninhibited Roman hospitality as much as for the food.

CARCIOFI ALLA GIUDIA

(Jewish fried artichokes)

BY DA ENZO AL 29

SERVES 4

1 lemon

4 Romanesco or globe artichokes

extra virgin olive oil, for frying

salt, for sprinkling

First, prepare the artichokes. Fill a large bowl with cold water, squeeze in the lemon juice and add the lemon rind.

Trim the artichokes by removing the tough outer leaves, then cutting off the top quarter of the head and removing another few layers of leaves. Trim the stalks, leaving about 6 cm (2½ inches) attached, and also remove the outer layer of the stem using a knife or vegetable peeler. Cut out the hairy choke (see Note) and use a spoon to clean out any fibrous spikes.

Once trimmed, immediately put the artichokes into the lemon water to stop them turning black. Leave to soak for at least 10 minutes.

To cook the artichokes, heat plenty of olive oil (enough to completely cover the artichokes) in a large heavy-based saucepan until it is very hot, but not quite boiling — about 150°C (300°F) on a cooking thermometer. Drain the artichokes well, removing any excess water by dabbing them with paper towel, then carefully immerse them into the oil. Cook for 8–10 minutes, or until they start to turn golden, moving them about regularly to ensure an even colour. Test if they are ready by pushing a toothpick into the base of the stem; if it is soft, the artichokes are ready.

Remove the artichokes with a slotted spoon and stand them upright on paper towel to cool and drain for at least 20 minutes.

When you are ready to serve the artichokes, use a fork to separate the leaves slightly and to encourage them to open out during the second frying. Sprinkle them with a little water to help them crisp up during their second frying.

Reheat the oil until boiling, then fry the artichokes for 1–2 minutes, or until the leaves are golden and crispy. Remove, drain again on paper towel, sprinkle with salt and serve immediately.

 NOTE: In Rome, *mammole* or Romanesco artichokes are used, and these do not have a hairy choke. If using a different variety, the centre will need to be removed.

In Rome, it's pretty hard to have a conversation about food without artichokes coming up. They are traditionally cooked two ways: *alla romana* (see page 125), and this fried version, known as the Jewish-style artichoke, and the most famous dish of Roman-Jewish cuisine. While it features on menus across Rome's Jewish Ghetto, this dish has also long infiltrated mainstream Roman cuisine. Traditionally Romanesco or *mammole* artichokes are used, but outside of Rome, globe artichokes will work just fine. The trick is that they are double fried — the first time to cook them through, and the second time to give the leaves that extra crisp and nutty crunch. This isn't a dish you can pre-prepare, but must be eaten fresh out of the fryer after sprinkling with salt.

CARBONARA

BY DA ENZO AL 29

SERVES 6

700 g (1 lb 9 oz) rigatoni

350 g (12½ oz) guanciale (cured pork cheek)

4 whole eggs

2 egg yolks

300 g (10½ oz) Pecorino Romano, grated, plus extra to serve

There isn't a dish debated more in Rome than *carbonara*. It is to Rome what *pizza* is to Naples, that is, iconic — and, traditionalists will say, untouchable. Nowadays you can find many chefs in Rome experimenting with ingredients and often adding a seasonal twist like asparagus or artichokes, but for me, nothing beats the classic. Everyone has an opinion on the matter; ask any Roman about where to eat a good *carbonara* and they will tell you only *their* choice is the best in town.

A few things to note about real-deal Roman *carbonara*: under no circumstance does it contain cream. Don't let even the creamiest one you try in the Eternal City mislead you. It's made with crispy *guanciale* (cured pork cheek), *pecorino* cheese and eggs. In Rome, it is unlike any *carbonara* you'll taste elsewhere, but recreating it at home is easy, with a lot of practice. The difference between a smooth one, and scrambled egg on pasta, is merely a matter of seconds. In fact, a chef once told me, 'Carbonara is a lot like life. If you're not watching closely, you'll screw it up!'

This recipe is from my favourite *trattoria* in Trastevere, Da Enzo al 29. Their version rarely disappoints, because it has just the right amount of saltiness and is decadently silky.

Bring a large saucepan of salted water to the boil. Add the pasta and cook for the time indicated on the packet.

Meanwhile, remove any rind from the guanciale and cut the meat into chunky strips about 1 cm (½ inch) thick.

Place a large frying pan over high heat, add the guanciale and fry for 4–5 minutes, or until the fat melts and the meat becomes crunchy.

Meanwhile, beat the eggs and egg yolks well until smooth, then mix in the pecorino and season with a generous grind of black pepper.

Once the pasta is *al dente*, drain and add to the pan with the guanciale, stirring well to coat the pasta in the guanciale fat.

Turn off the heat. If you are feeling confident, add the egg mixture to the pan, tossing the ingredients together rapidly to avoid the egg scrambling. Alternatively, the foolproof method is to add the pasta and guanciale into the bowl with the eggs and stir well. The heat from the pasta will cook the egg and the sauce will remain silky smooth.

Serve with a sprinkling of pecorino and a good grind of black pepper.

 NOTE: In Italy, *carbonara* is usually prepared with 'pasta gialla' eggs, a special type of local egg with an intense yellow yolk, which gives the dish a distinctive yellow colour. Regular eggs will create a paler *carbonara*, but the flavour will still be the same.

MARIA CHIARA DI FELICE

DA ENZO AL 29 TRATTORIA

Da Enzo al 29 in Trastevere is my neighbourhood go-to *trattoria*. It's your picture-perfect Roman *trattoria*, located on one of the quieter streets of a *quartiere* that is laden with restaurants targeting tourists. For me, Da Enzo is paper tablecloths that adorn tables positioned for a tight squeeze, the friendliest and most knowledgeable staff, and a *burrata* cheese that is irresistible. It is tiny, family-run and bursting at the seams on any given night. As I arrive they put aside my favourite dessert because, in the past, they've seen the look of devastation on my face when they have run out before I could order it.

Da Enzo opened in 1935 and the Di Felice family took it over in 1988. It was already a neighbourhood institution, and they have continued to do the place justice. Maria Chiara manages the *trattoria* with her two brothers and a team of dedicated staff. She says, 'What we do here is focus on simplicity. Every day we honour the Roman culinary traditions of the past; the ones we have inherited.'

They use only the best local ingredients from small producers. In fact, Maria Chiara talks fondly of the family trips they take into the Roman and even Abruzzo countryside where, as soon as they see a 'farm' sign on the road, they stop to check what produce is on offer and to explore potential partnerships. 'You get to see another side of Italy when you delve into the regions and country towns. It's where many artisans are hidden away, following production practices of years gone by,' she says.

'What they do speaks to our philosophy of providing our customers not only with high-quality ingredients, but things that are organic and not mass- or over-produced.' Maria Chiara speaks nostalgically about Roman cuisine, *la cucina Romana*. 'It is a gastronomic masterpiece born from the working class. It's simple and calls for an appreciation of locally grown food.'

While the concept of a casual restaurant such as the *trattoria* dates back to Roman times, it existed more so in the format of an *osteria*. Here one would go to drink, socialise and relax after a hard day's work. You would bring your own food, because *osterie* didn't have kitchens. While places like this exist around the world, Maria Chiara insists that the Roman *trattoria* (the modern version of an *osteria*) is unique. 'It has its own identity and place within the Roman psyche. It is where Roman

families go for their sacred Sunday lunch, where friends gather for dinner and where you indulge in a hot dish and glass of wine on a lunch break instead of grabbing a quick *panino*. It's where you know your waiter's name and they know yours, and where you're made to feel at home.'

And this is what Da Enzo embodies. Their *trattoria* has hardly changed since the 1930s, other than some aesthetic repairs and updates. It's a tiny space, but the Di Felice family have no intentions to expand. Maria Chiara says this authenticity is what keeps clients coming back for more: 'People know that they'll get a great meal in an atmosphere that is family-orientated, friendly, but above all, real.'

The Di Felice family is proud of their heritage and the honour bestowed on them to share Roman traditions with locals and foreigners alike. Maria Chiara says the Eternal City is their inspiration. 'Rome gave birth to the modern world. And while it is disorganised, chaotic and, quite often, extremely difficult to live with, it's as stunning as a film set.'

She quotes Russian novelist Fyodor Dostoevsky: 'If "beauty will save the world", then Rome will save us all until the end of time.'

AMATRICIANA

BY ELEONORA CHIARI

SERVES 4

150 g (5½ oz) guanciale (cured pork cheek)

1 red chilli

400 g (14 oz) rigatoni, mezze maniche or bucatini pasta

2 tablespoons extra virgin olive oil

350 g (12½ oz) fresh cherry tomatoes, chopped (or tinned chopped tomatoes)

50 g (1¾ oz) Pecorino Romano, grated, plus extra for serving

50 g (1¾ oz) Parmigiano Reggiano, grated, plus extra to serve

Heat a large frying pan. Cut the guanciale into chunky strips about 1 cm (½ inch) thick and add them to the pan with the whole chilli. Fry over medium heat for about 2–3 minutes, or until the guanciale becomes dark and crunchy and the fat has melted. Turn off the heat.

Remove the guanciale using a slotted spoon and drain on paper towel. Discard the chilli, but leave the leftover fat in the frying pan.

Bring a large saucepan of salted water to the boil. Add the pasta and cook for the time indicated on the packet.

Meanwhile, add the olive oil to the leftover guanciale fat, then add the tomatoes. Season with salt and freshly ground black pepper and cook over low heat for 10 minutes.

Once the pasta is *al dente*, drain and add to the sauce, along with the cooked guanciale. Mix everything together, then turn off the heat and stir the pecorino and parmigiano through.

Serve with an extra sprinkling of cheese.

The tomato-based *amatriciana* is a Roman favourite, although its origins lie in the Lazio town of Amatrice, hence the name. In Rome, unlike what might be served up outside of Italy, *amatriciana* is made with *pecorino* cheese, tomato and *guanciale* (cured pork cheek). My friend Eleonora is seven generations Roman (in Rome you aren't considered Roman unless your bloodline dates back at least seven generations!), and her *amatriciana* is to die for, yet she defies tradition by adding some *Parmigiano Reggiano* and a hint of chilli.

You can stick with her version, or play around with this to make it your own. Serve it with either *rigatoni, mezze maniche* or *bucatini* pasta.

CACIO E PEPE

BY ALBA ESTEVE RUIZ, MARZAPANE

SERVES 6

360 g (12½ oz) tonnarelli, spaghetti or spaghettoni

320 g (11½ oz) Pecorino Romano, grated, plus extra to serve

120 g (4½ oz) Parmigiano Reggiano, grated

2 teaspoons freshly ground black pepper

Every time I explain *cacio e pepe* to visitors dining with me in Rome, I find myself trying to convince them it isn't boring. Pasta with *cacio* (Roman dialect for 'cheese' — in this case *pecorino*) and *pepe* ('pepper') doesn't sound all that inviting, but a *cacio e pepe* done well will seduce you with its sharp and salty creaminess. Chef Alba Esteve Ruiz, of Rome's popular Marzapane restaurant, kindly shared her recipe with me. This young, award-winning chef moved to Rome from Alicante in Spain, having kickstarted her career at none other than Girona's El Celler de Can Roca — the three Michelin star restaurant which has also held the mantle for the world's best restaurant.

The key to making this dish work is to keep the cheese at room temperature, and to mix it well with the right amount of water that you boiled your pasta in; some chefs encourage you to add pasta water to the cheese and pepper mix to make a paste of sorts. Ultimately, it is a dish that requires a bit of practice. Alba adds *Parmigiano Reggiano* to her dish, but if you prefer, sticking with the traditional *pecorino* is totally fine, and while *tonnarelli* are customary in Rome, serving it with *spaghetti* or *spaghettoni* would do just as well at home.

Bring a large saucepan of salted water to the boil. Add the pasta and cook for the time indicated on the packet.

Meanwhile, in a large bowl, mix together the pecorino, parmigiano and black pepper.

Once the pasta is al dente, drain and add to the cheese mixture, reserving the cooking water.

Mix well, then gradually stir through 4–5 tablespoons of the extra cooking water, a spoonful at a time, until the cheese melts and the sauce coats the pasta.

If the sauce is too dry, add a little more water and continue to stir until smooth.

Serve with an extra grind of black pepper and an extra sprinkling of pecorino.

SIGNOR ROBERTO

I stumbled across my local cheese shop in Trastevere — Antica Caciara — in my first few months in Rome. I never had my own 'cheese shop' in Australia. As I approached, I could literally smell it before I could see it.

Walking into this unassuming store, you find it's all you would expect from an Italian neighbourhood delicatessen — from the hanging *salumi* and the wheels of *Pecorino Romano*, to the warm family welcome you receive at the door. Roberto Pollica and his wife, Anna, work here every day with a couple of other staff members. They never prepare my cheese order without asking what I need it for, who's coming for dinner and what else is on the menu, so that they can perfectly select some of that golden goodness for me.

But Antica Caciara is more than just 'a cheese shop'. And not just for me, but for the *Trasteverini*, Romans, suppliers and clients who travel across the city to buy from Signor Roberto. It's a place filled with history, passion and love.

In 1900 Roberto's *nonno* Albino opened the store, and eventually his father Antonio took it over. At 13 years old, Roberto began working to help out his dad. That was in 1963 and he has worked every single day since. He told me, 'At that age I could never have imagined it would become my life — nor did I have the maturity to know if I wanted it to.'

In the early 1970s, after his father passed away, he found himself with a shop to manage, staff twice his age and a growing challenge with the rise of supermarkets in Rome. With similar specialty stores struggling, his staff, fearful of losing their jobs, tried to convince him to modernise — to start stocking household detergents, baby food and nappies, lower-quality and cheaper cheeses.

But the need he felt to honour his grandfather's and father's dream was too strong so, even though he himself wasn't confident about the future, he took a risk and held steadfast. 'Somehow we made it through. What I learnt was that if you believe in something, then don't ever listen to anyone, just follow your instinct.' Roberto says he won't let his father's passion die. After all, this is not just a job for him, but a profound family calling.

It doesn't matter who you are, when you walk into Antica Caciara, you receive that old-school, one-on-one treatment that is so hard to find nowadays. This couple — happily married for 40 years — truly treat you like their own. Signor Roberto has also resisted putting in a number system like most delicatessens. He says, 'Everywhere you go, you have to take a number. At the bank, the pharmacy; you're just a number. Well in my shop you are a customer. I respect and treat everyone well; people are more than just a number for me.'

And this love he has for his customers is reciprocated. Everyone in the neighbourhood smiles when you mention Signor Roberto. Together with Anna, they are local legends.

Signor Roberto says he is one of a handful of specialty shops in Trastevere to have lasted so long. The secret to his success and longevity?

'You have to love it. But *really* love it. If you're in this business just to focus on the profit, you've already lost.'

In 2016 and 2017, when some of their *salumi* and pork suppliers in earthquake-ravaged Umbria slowed or even halted production, Signor Roberto alleviated their concerns, telling them he would not abandon them and would not restock until they were back on their feet. He said, 'I would rather run out of stock and lose money than go to other suppliers and compromise the quality and consistency of what I sell. That's customer service, that's business — putting *their* interests before financial ones.'

When I go in each week to buy my cheese, I always secretly hope Signor Roberto serves me, because his smile and generosity have the ability to turn your day around.

I tell him what I'd like and he replies with his famous, *'Ci penso io tesoro!'* ('Leave it to me, sweetheart!'). He gives me a couple of tastings, and then a kiss goodbye, too.

LA GRICIA

BY ANGELO PREZIOSI

SERVES 4

350 g (12½ oz) rigatoni

300 g (10½ oz) guanciale (cured pork cheek)

125 ml (4 fl oz/½ cup) dry white wine

100 g (3½ oz) Pecorino Romano, grated

The first time I tried *la gricia*, I had just moved to Rome and was lunching with my dad's childhood friend, Peppe. His nephew was the chef, and came to take our order. He asked me if I liked *amatriciana*. I said yes, but would prefer something without tomato sauce. He responded, 'Well what about *la gricia* — it's a white *amatriciana*.'

And so began my love for *la gricia*. It's lighter than a *carbonara* because it doesn't have eggs in it. Again, the trick here is to use the water your pasta has boiled in to mix with the cheese and make a silky, smooth sauce.

This is a family recipe from my Roman friend, Angelo. The salty, crispy *guanciale* (cured pork cheek) with the sharpness of the *pecorino* is a match made in heaven.

Bring a large saucepan of salted water to the boil. Add the pasta and cook for almost the length of time indicated on the packet.

Meanwhile, trim any rind from the guanciale and cut the meat into chunky strips about 1 cm (½ inch) wide.

Heat a frying pan and add the guanciale. Cook over medium heat for 2–3 minutes, or until the guanciale turns crispy and releases its fat. Turn up the heat, pour in the wine and simmer for a couple of minutes to reduce.

One minute before the end of the instructed cooking time, drain the pasta and add to the frying pan, along with 3–4 tablespoons of its cooking water. Mix everything together and continue to cook over medium heat until the pasta is *al dente*.

Turn off the heat and stir in the pecorino to thicken the sauce. Add a generous grind of black pepper and serve immediately.

Many food purists say seafood and cheese don't mix. In my family, you never saw cheese on the table if pasta with fish was being served, and in Italy, if you were to ask for it at a restaurant after having ordered *spaghetti alle vongole* or *risotto alla crema di scampi* you'd just about get arrested. Yet, the memo seems to have been missed with this dish in Rome. Gnocchi with a *pecorino* cheese and mussel sauté is on the menu at many Roman *trattorie*, and it's some sort of a divine match.

My friend Angelo's gnocchi — his paternal Nonna Stella's recipe — is just perfect. He'd come home from school at lunchtime and she would ask what he'd like to eat. When he said gnocchi, she would roll up her sleeves and make them from scratch. You can use Angelo's gnocchi recipe to match with any sauce you like, especially leftover sauce from your *coda alla vaccinara* (see page 179), which is one of my favourites.

It's a delicious dish any day of the week, but why not do as the Romans do and make Thursdays 'gnocchi day' at your house too!

GNOCCHI COZZE E PECORINO

(Gnocchi with mussels and pecorino)

BY ANGELO PREZIOSI

SERVES 4

1 kg (2 lb 3 oz) mussels

100 ml (3½ fl oz) olive oil

2 garlic cloves, peeled

1 small bunch Italian
(flat-leaf) parsley,
roughly chopped

100 g (3½ oz) Pecorino
Romano, grated

Gnocchi

500 g (1 lb 2 oz) floury/
boiling potatoes

1 egg, beaten

250 g (9 oz/1⅔ cups) plain
(all-purpose) flour, plus
extra for dusting

pinch of freshly grated
nutmeg

3 tablespoons grated
Parmigiano Reggiano

To make the gnocchi, rinse the whole, unpeeled potatoes and place them in a large saucepan of cold water with a pinch of salt. Bring to the boil and cook at a rapid boil for about 30 minutes, or until just tender. Drain and leave to cool, then remove the skins.

Mash the potatoes and mix together in a bowl with the beaten egg, flour, nutmeg and parmigiano. On a bench, knead with your hands to obtain a smooth dough. If the mixture is too sticky, add a little more flour; if it is too dry add a splash of water.

Divide the dough into four pieces and roll each into a long sausage shape, about 2 cm (¾ inch) thick. With a sharp knife, cut the logs into pieces about 2 cm (¾ inch) long, to make little square pillows. Place the gnocchi on a tray dusted with flour and sprinkle with a little more flour. Set aside while you prepare the sauce.

Rinse the mussels and remove the hairy beards; discard any that are broken or open. In a large frying pan, heat the olive oil and gently fry the garlic until soft. Add the mussels and cover. Cook over high heat for 4–5 minutes, or until they begin to open.

When all the mussels have opened, turn off the heat, remove the mussels from the pan and strain the remaining juices through a fine sieve, adding the strained juices back to the pan. Remove the shells from all but 24 mussels. Put all the mussels back into the sauce and reheat over medium heat.

Meanwhile, bring a large saucepan of salted water to the boil. Slowly add all the gnocchi to the boiling water and cook for about 1–2 minutes, until they rise back up to the surface.

Scoop out the gnocchi using a slotted spoon and add to the mussels. Turn off the heat and stir in the parsley.

Serve each dish topped with six mussels still in their shells, and a generous sprinkling of pecorino.

ABBACCHIO ALLO SCOTTADITO
(Grilled lamb cutlets)

BY PIERO DRAGO AND JACOPO RICCI, SECONDO TRADIZIONE

SERVES 4

1 garlic clove, crushed

2 tablespoons wild thyme

60 ml (2 fl oz/¼ cup) extra virgin olive oil

20 suckling lamb chops and cutlets (about 1 kg/ 2 lb 3 oz)

Abbacchio is Roman dialect for 'lamb', and *scottadito* means 'burn your fingers', which kind of paints the picture for this dish, found in every single *trattoria* in Rome and regional Lazio. Lamb cutlets, usually dressed with a little rosemary, salt, pepper and oil, are flame-grilled, and you're supposed to eat them smoking hot, while trying not to burn those fingers.

This recipe is by young chefs Piero Drago and Jacopo Ricci, of Secondo Tradizione. They came to this stylish bistro after working at the two-Michelin starred Il Pagliaccio, and their repertoire is about the Roman classics — refined without being pretentious. So they've added a twist and used thyme instead of rosemary. Feel free to go either way. The important thing is to let the cutlets marinate so that the flavour is infused.

In a large bowl, mix together the garlic, thyme and olive oil. Add the lamb and mix well to coat the meat with the marinade. Cover and leave in the fridge for at least 2 hours.

Remove the lamb from the fridge 30 minutes before cooking, to bring it to room temperature, and season well with salt.

Heat a heavy frying pan or chargrill pan until very hot. Add the lamb and fry over high heat until browned but still pink and tender in the middle — about 3–4 minutes on each side, depending on the size of the pieces.

Serve immediately and eat with your hands.

NOTE: Typically *abbacchio* is a baby milk-fed lamb (under 6 kg/13 lb), and *agnello* is an older lamb, weighing 7–10 kg (15–22 lb). Outside of Italy, *agnello* is more common, so you can use larger lamb chops but adjust the cooking time.

The classic *secondo* course of the *cucina Romana* repertoire is pan-fried veal with salty *prosciutto* and crisp sage. My friend Eleonora gave me this recipe, and having grown up in Rome, she sure knows her Roman food. Add TV host, journalist and co-owner of custom food tour specialists, Casa Mia Italy Food & Wine, and her experience is hard to beat.

'The key to *saltimbocca*,' Eleonora explains, 'is keeping it bite-sized, and not overcooking. They're called "jump in the mouth" for a reason.'

Soak up all the pan juices with some fresh bread (do *'la scarpetta'* as we say in Rome), and if you can get your hands on it, Eleonora says to pair this dish with the famous Lazio red, *Cesanese*.

SALTIMBOCCA ALLA ROMANA

(Pan-fried veal with prosciutto and sage)

BY ELEONORA BALDWIN

SERVES 4

12 thinly sliced lean veal cutlets, about 500 g (1 lb 2 oz), at room temperature

60 g (2 oz) prosciutto, sliced wafer-thin

1 bunch fresh sage

50 g (1¾ oz/⅓ cup) plain (all-purpose) flour

50 g (1¾ oz) unsalted butter

125 ml (4 fl oz/½ cup) dry white wine

Using scissors, remove any fat or sinew from the veal, then cut each slice in half to make 24 bite-sized pieces.

Cut the prosciutto roughly the same size as the veal and lay a piece on top of each cutlet. Top each one with a small sage leaf (or half a large one). Fasten the prosciutto and sage to the veal using a toothpick, and lightly dust each cutlet with flour on both sides.

Heat the butter in a wide frying pan and add the cutlets. Cook over medium–high heat for a minute, then turn the cutlets over and pour in the wine to deglaze the pan.

Cook for another 2 minutes, turning regularly to cook evenly on both sides — but be careful not to overcook, or the prosciutto will become tough and leathery.

Season the *saltimbocca* to taste and serve immediately, with plenty of bread to mop up the sauce.

STRACOTTO

(Slow-cooked Jewish beef stew)

SERVES 4

100 ml (3½ fl oz) extra
virgin olive oil

1 kg (2 lb 3 oz) piece of
boneless beef, such as
chuck or brisket

1 onion, finely sliced

1.4 litres (47 fl oz) tomato
passata (puréed tomatoes)

Stracotto literally means 'overcooked', and nothing says comfort food like this dish of the Roman-Jewish repertoire. This slow-cooked beef in a rich tomato sauce was traditionally cooked on a Friday to be eaten on Shabbat, when cooking wasn't allowed — so the best part about it is that it can be prepared ahead, then reheated the following day. Its beauty also lies in the fact that it cooks away for hours on the stove without too much attention.

While it was historically served as a main-course dish, nowadays, once the meat has been eaten, the leftover flavourful sauce is used for pasta. In the home, Roman Jews might have *stracotto* for Friday night dinner or Shabbat lunch. It's simple to prepare, and has few ingredients, but will make quite an impression. It's best served with something fresh on the side, like a salad, or in Rome with *puntarelle* (see page 116).

Heat the olive oil in a large saucepan. Season the beef with salt and pepper, then place in the pan along with the onion. Brown the meat over medium–high heat for about 8–10 minutes, turning to ensure all sides are sealed.

Add the passata, stirring well. Cover the pan and leave to cook over low heat for 3 hours, stirring every 30 minutes. If the sauce begins to reduce too much and dry out, add 250 ml (8½ fl oz/1 cup) of water.

At the end of the cooking time, the meat should be tender and falling apart, and the sauce should be thick and rich.

Season to taste, then slice the beef into pieces to serve, keeping aside any leftover sauce for pasta.

FORMAGGIO

It's not uncommon in Italy — and Rome is no exception — to have your own cheese supplier or a regular stall at the local market where you purchase your cheese. Roberto Pollica and his wife Anna of Antica Caciara, in Trastevere, are my local cheesemongers and, in just a few years, have taught me much about cheese — the easy way, by tasting it. Roberto has stocked hundreds of cheeses over the years and says the only way you can get to know cheese is by tasting it until you find the textures and flavours you like.

While *Parmigiano Reggiano* is often touted as the king of all cheeses, in Rome, *Pecorino Romano* is the dairy drug of choice. And Anna says that foreigners are pleasantly surprised when they taste its delicate flavour, having instead expected something quite strong and overbearing.

There isn't a Roman household, *trattoria* or chef who isn't in possession of this sheep's milk cheese, which is used on dishes from *carbonara* to *amatriciana* to the old classic of *trippa all romana* (tripe).

THE ROLE OF CHEESE IN ROME

Italy is consistently in the top five global cheese producers and exporters. However, Eleonora Baldwin, an American-born and Italian-raised TV host, journalist and culinary connoisseur based in Rome, says the actual number of varieties is difficult to quantify. 'There is no exact number,' explains the co-owner of culinary tour company Casa Mia Italy Food and Wine. 'Italy churns, blends, pulls, stretches and ages milk into virtually thousands of different cheese varieties. Each region, city and hamlet is home to ridiculous amounts of native *formaggi*.'

And Eleonora goes on to say that *cucina Romana* couldn't exist without it. 'Here, cheese doesn't play the starring role — rather it is the key character actor whose brilliant performance completes the Oscar-winning film. Think of *carbonara*, *amatriciana*, *la gricia* and *cacio e pepe* without *pecorino*. Impossible! In this case, cheese is what shapes

the umami element, bringing saltiness and creamy texture to the dishes.'

Even when you look beyond the Roman pasta foursome, you'll find cheese everywhere. Typical snacks like *supplì* have a melting mozzarella centre, *ravioli* are filled with fresh ricotta, *mozzarelline* are crumbed and fried mozzarella found on every *pizzeria* menu, and *mozzarella in carrozza* are like hot mozzarella sandwiches. And as spring approaches, on 1 May (the May Day holiday, celebrating workers) Romans typically head out of town for a picnic with family and friends, and eat, among other things, *pecorino* and *fave* (broad beans). The pairing is easy, inexpensive and easy to transport. Traditions like these date back to Roman times, but continue to be honoured today.

DINING AND CHEESE IN ROME

At a *trattoria*, wine bar or at *aperitivo* time, it's very common to find *taglieri* on the menu. This is the Italian word for 'chopping board', and here it refers to a cheese or *salumi* board. Eleonora says, 'Romans are very proud of their sheep's milk dairy products, *Ricotta di Pecora* and *Pecorino Romano*. Ricotta, however, is technically not cheese! No rennet is used to make ricotta; it is simply whey that's been cooked twice (re-cooked = ri-cotta).' While ricotta can be made with cow's, goat's or even buffalo milk, *la ricotta Romana* is made with sheep's milk.

Some other less common cheeses that have started to grow in popularity in Rome are *conciato* (herb-infused and semi-aged in ancient Roman terracotta amphorae) and *caciofiore della Campagna Romana*, an all-vegetarian product where animal rennet is replaced by soaked wild thistles, a technique that dates back to the 1st century. Others include *caciottine* and *provole* (pressed or stretched-curd artisan cheeses common in central and south Italy), *fiocco della tuscia* (brie-like and made in nearby Viterbo), and local *mozzarella di bufala* (made from free-range milk from buffaloes that graze in Lazio's Pontine marshlands).

Over the years, cheeses from other Italian regions have snuck over the border and are now commonly found all over the country. Products like *ricotta salata* (a hard ricotta from Sicily that has been pressed, salted and dried), *Parmigiano Reggiano* (from the north, and only considered certified if it's produced in five particular cities, mainly in Emilia–Romagna), buffalo mozzarella (from the Campania region) and deliciously creamy *burrata* (a mozzarella filled with cream), which hails from Puglia.

PECORINO ROMANO VS PECORINO

Growing up in Rome, Eleonora says the perfume of *Pecorino Romano* nostalgically reminds her of her childhood. While *pecorino* is produced all over Italy from Sardinia to Abruzzo, Le Marche to Tuscany, *Pecorino Romano* is DOP — *Denominazione di Origine Protetta*, the Italian term for the European Union system law that protects the names of specialty food products with a specific geographic origin.

The art of cheese making in Rome can be traced back thousands of years. From 500BC to 400AD, legions of Roman soldiers travelled with herds of sheep to guarantee a wholesome and constant supply of *pecorino* cheese. 'Because of its long shelf life and protein-rich nutrients, soldiers' daily rations consisted of 27 grams of *pecorino*, a chunk of bread and a bowl of spelt soup to provide them with the energy to march long distances,' says Eleonora.

Eleonora says that nowadays 90% of the milk for *pecorino* comes from Sardinia, and while production techniques have evolved, they remain quite similar to those of 2000 years ago. She explains, 'The processing of *Pecorino Romano* DOP — limited to Lazio, Sardinia and the province of Grosseto in Tuscany — is the result of centuries of honed experience, where basic steps are still entrusted to the hands and experience of the cheese maker. What sets savoury, crumbly *Pecorino Romano* apart from other regional, more elastic, often milder *pecorino* is its unique, compact texture and assertive, yet carefully balanced, salty character.'

BUYING AND CONSERVING CHEESE

Ask

Any good cheesemonger will be able to talk cheese for hours. Ask questions, tell them what you like, and what you intend to do with the cheese — is it for cooking, or for a cheese board?

Taste

Only by tasting many cheeses will you find the ones you like (and dislike).

Dare

Try cheeses you normally wouldn't. You'll find that even blue cheeses aren't all equal, and the flavour may be more delicate than the scent. Try cheeses filled with berries or honey, nuts and even wine-soaked dried fruits.

Pair

Cheese pairs perfectly with wine and other foods, such as nuts, fruit, bread, jams, honey and chutneys. Again, ask for advice on what goes with what.

Wrap

At home, parchment paper is a good short-term option for wrapping your cheese in, but for longevity, cheesecloth (muslin) is recommended. Storing it under a cheese dome (*campana di vetro*) is ideal; be aware that keeping cheese in plastic wrap for an extended period of time can stop the cheese 'breathing' and encourage mould to form.

PREPARING THE PERFECT CHEESE BOARD

Board

A wooden, marble or slate board works best.

Variety

The number of cheeses doesn't matter nearly as much as the range. Ensure you balance origin (region, country), milk type, colour, texture (soft vs hard) and flavour.

Star attraction

Cheese can be expensive, so why not make an impression by spending a little extra on just one of your pieces, and that one will be the star of the show.

Temperature

Serve cheese at room temperature. It should be taken out of the refrigerator 1–2 hours prior to serving, and can be left in its wrapping or cloth until you start eating.

The clock

Following an imaginary clock (*l'orologio*) on your board, arrange your cheeses clockwise, starting from the most delicate (usually your young, soft cheeses) to hard cheese and blue cheese.

Cut

Each cheese is handled and cut differently. For instance, cheese with an edible crust should be cut into slices; *Parmigiano Reggiano* should be crumbled. Provide the appropriate knife for each cheese, especially to avoid contamination. And to avoid any confusion, any inedible crusts should be removed.

Accompaniments

Provide some contrast on your board. Always add something crunchy (nuts), sweet (honey, jam, fresh or dried fruit), and something neutral (bread or water crackers). A quick rule of thumb is fresh fruit for soft cheese, dried fruit for hard cheese, and jams, preserves, marmalades and honey for anything strong. Avoid anything sour or salty like pickled vegetables or *salumi*. And wine pairs well too!

Etiquette

Whoever serves the cheese board (generally the host) will indicate the cheese starting point.

semi-aged caciotta

pecorino romano

pecorino di
pienza

robiola

gorgonzola

buffalo
mozzarella

smoked scamorza

TIRAMISÙ

BY TONI BRANCATISANO

SERVES 6

350 ml (12 fl oz) strong black coffee

3 eggs

pinch of salt

100 g (3½ oz) caster (superfine) sugar

1 tablespoon Marsala or rum (optional)

300 g (10½ oz) mascarpone

1 packet savoiardi (lady finger biscuits)

unsweetened cocoa powder, for dusting

chocolate-coated coffee beans, to serve (optional)

The origins of the *tiramisù* (Italian for 'pick-me-up') continue to be debated, with most historical accounts suggesting it was first made in the Veneto region. Its simplicity and deliciousness has seen it transcend borders, locally and internationally, and it has basically become Italy's national dessert. Found in *pasticcerie*, restaurants and *trattorie*, *tiramisù* is super easy to make at home, and I've made it countless times since childhood. Like this recipe from my friend Toni — Italian-Australian TV host and pastry cook extraordinaire — my mum would soak her biscuits in a liquor-scented coffee, but I always make mine without. Toni says *tiramisù* is great because it can be made a day or two ahead, and is versatile in that you can assemble it in a large bowl or baking dish, or individually in glasses or cups.

First, make the coffee and set aside to cool completely.

Separate the eggs, putting the yolks and whites in two separate bowls. Add a pinch of salt to the egg whites and whisk with an electric mixer until soft peaks begin to form. Add half the sugar, 1 tablespoon at a time, until it is all incorporated and the mixture is white, aerated and glossy. Set aside.

Add the remaining sugar to the egg yolks and beat until they are pale and fluffy, and the sugar has dissolved. Add the Marsala, if using, then slowly incorporate the mascarpone on a low speed.

Using a spoon, fold half the egg whites into the yolk mixture. Continue gently stirring in the remaining egg whites, being careful not to knock out all the air. If not using immediately, cover and keep in the fridge until needed.

Dip the biscuits quickly into the coffee, then use them to line the bottom of whichever serving bowl, dish or cups you are using. Spoon over a layer of mascarpone cream. Repeat to make two or three more layers, ending with a layer of mascarpone.

Dust with a generous sprinkling of cocoa powder, then decorate, if you like, with chocolate-coated coffee beans.

MOUSSE DI MASCARPONE CON FRAGOLINE DI BOSCO

(Mascarpone mousse with wild strawberries)

BY DA ENZO AL 29

SERVES 6

3 eggs

3 tablespoons caster (superfine) sugar

400 g (14 oz) mascarpone

300 g (10½ oz) wild strawberries (or regular strawberries, quartered)

icing (confectioners') sugar, for dusting

The mascarpone mousse with *fragoline di bosco* (wild strawberries) at Da Enzo is my favourite dessert in Rome. It might sound like a big call, and it is. But it's the truth. When I walk in and even before I sit down, I ask whoever's working that day — whether it be owners Francesco, Roberto, Maria Chiara or one of their cute waiters — to put one aside for me. They only make a set number each day, and I can't face a meal here without knowing there's a mousse waiting for me.

They shared this divine recipe with me, and I hope it will sweeten your dinner parties for years to come. If you can't source *fragoline di bosco*, regular strawberries will work fine, as will any other berry.

Place the eggs and sugar into the bowl of an electric mixer and start beating at medium speed.

Once the mixture turns pale yellow, add the mascarpone, set the speed to high and mix until the consistency turns thick and dense.

Spoon a few tablespoons of strawberries into each serving glass and cover with the mascarpone cream. Top with another spoonful of strawberries.

Refrigerate for at least an hour, before serving with a sprinkling of icing sugar.

Chapter Two

LA FRIGG

ITORIA

La friggitoria translates literally to the 'fried food shop'. Italians can agree that the *friggitoria* has its origins in Naples, the home of the fry — but they are found all over Italy.

When in Rome, the smell of freshly fried *supplì* (fried rice balls) and *filetti di baccalà* (battered and fried salt cod fillets) will lure you in off those cobblestone streets. *Supplì*, *filetti di baccalà*, *fiori di zucca* (battered and fried mozzarella and anchovy-stuffed zucchini flowers) are just some of the treats you'll find in what are usually little hole-in-the wall places. Croquettes, *mozzarelline* (fried mozzarella balls), and even *olive ascolane* (stuffed, crumbed and fried olives) are also on the list, which just goes on. My neighbourhood *friggitoria* is called I Supplì, which gives you a pretty clear idea as to what they specialise in.

The *supplì* is to Romans what the *arancino* is to Sicilians. But don't ever make the mistake of referring to one as the other in the Eternal City because you may very well offend. And the truth is, they are distinctively different. The Roman *supplì* is generally oval, and the classic version is tomato-based risotto stuffed with mozzarella, then crumbed and deep fried. When you crack one open the mozzarella oozes into strings like a telephone cord, which is why Romans call them *supplì al telefono*.

While the latest buzzword on the international foodie scene is 'street food', it is by no means a new concept in Rome. The things I see in food outlets today touted as street food (*panino con porchetta*, *pizza rossa*, *fritti*) have been staples almost forever. In fact they make up childhood memories

I formed on my first visit to Italy in the 1980s. Here in Rome, street food applies to anything you can eat on the run, standing at a bar, or literally on the street. Quick and generally inexpensive, it has become even more popular and inventive since the economic crisis of the last decade really started to hit Italian household budgets.

Like many other *friggitorie* across town, I Supplì also serves up dishes you would find at a *tavola calda* (an Italian version of a cafe or cafeteria) — basically those that are eaten in the home; think pasta dishes, roast meats and baked vegetables. And given Italians come to trust their local vendors, they are confident in the fact that a cheap yet wholesome meal is guaranteed.

It really doesn't take long to develop meaningful rapport with Romans. They are renowned around Italy for being boisterous, friendly and open. Take Loreto and the boys at I Supplì for instance. Some of the staff I know by name, some just by face, but because I go so often, they notice when I've been away from Rome and always greet me with a smiling *Bentornata* ('Welcome back'). It's that which takes service to another level. They make you feel special and in a sense, part of the family.

I recall, especially in my first few months living in Rome when I didn't know many people, how it made me feel like I belonged and that I was part of this special community.

And community is one of the things I truly love most about Rome and Italy, because while things might not be perfect around here, passion and big hearts can be found all over.

SUPPLÌ
(Fried rice balls)

BY I SUPPLÌ, TRASTEVERE

If you had to pick one snack item that Romans love, it would have to be *supplì*. And God help anyone who refers to them as an *arancino*: *arancini* are Sicilian fried rice balls, and *supplì* are Roman. Their name comes from the French word for 'surprise', as they are filled with a gooey mozzarella centre. Roman kids might eat one as an after-school snack, and they are commonly seen on *pizzeria* menus as the customary *fritto* (fried starter) before pizza is served.

My favourite *supplì* is from I Supplì in Trastevere; they gave me their longtime recipe for what is known as one of the best in Rome.

MAKES 10

2 eggs

200 g (7 oz) fine dry breadcrumbs

extra virgin olive oil, for deep-frying

Rice filling

250 g (9 oz) tomatoes

3 tablespoons extra virgin olive oil

½ onion, finely diced

½ celery stalk, finely diced

50 g (1¾ oz) chicken livers, finely chopped

80 g (2¾ oz) minced (ground) beef

60 ml (2 fl oz/¼ cup) dry white wine

250 g (9 oz) Carnaroli or Arborio rice

500 ml (17 fl oz/2 cups) stock

1 egg, beaten

50 g (1¾ oz) fresh mozzarella

Start by preparing the rice filling. Peel the tomatoes by scoring a cross on the bottom of each one, put them in a heatproof bowl and cover with boiling water. Leave for 30 seconds, then move them to a bowl of cold water and remove the skins by peeling away from the cross. Cut the tomatoes in half and use a spoon to scoop out the seeds. Chop the tomatoes and set aside.

Heat the olive oil in a large saucepan and lightly sauté the onion and celery over medium heat until soft. Add the chicken livers and the beef and cook for about 5 minutes, or until browned all over. Stir in the wine and chopped tomatoes and season with salt and a good grind of black pepper.

Cover and leave to cook over low heat for about 10 minutes, or until the sauce begins to thicken. Add the rice and stock, stir well, and leave to cook for another 20 minutes, stirring occasionally, until the rice is *al dente*. If necessary, add a little more stock or water. The mixture should be thick and compact, similar to a risotto. Turn off the heat, stir in the beaten egg, then pour the mixture onto a large tray and leave to cool so the rice absorbs all of the sauce.

Meanwhile, dice the mozzarella into 1 cm (½ inch) cubes and place in a colander to drain away any excess liquid.

When the rice reaches room temperature, take a handful of the mixture, insert a cube of mozzarella and close the rice into an egg shape, being careful to ensure the cheese stays within the rice. Using your hands, press into an oval shape. Try to make all the other *supplì* a similar size and shape. Once formed, place on a tray covered with baking paper, ready for coating.

To coat the *supplì*, beat the eggs in a bowl and pour the breadcrumbs onto a large plate. Immerse each ball into the egg, then roll in the breadcrumbs, using your hands to compact the coating evenly. Once coated, put the *supplì* back onto the lined tray.

When all the *supplì* are prepared, fill a large saucepan with plenty of olive oil and heat until boiling — about 170°C (340°F) on a cooking thermometer.

Add the *supplì* to the oil one at a time, to avoid the temperature of the oil dropping, and fry in batches of two or three until golden, about 7–8 minutes, turning them regularly to ensure an even colour.

Drain on paper towel and serve hot, while the mozzarella centre is gooey and the coating is crispy.

LORETO BIZZARRI

I SUPPLÌ

On any day of the week you will have to line up at Trastevere's favourite *friggitoria*, I Supplì. Also a *rosticceria* (where you can buy roast meats, like chicken) and *pizza al taglio* (pizza by the slice) joint, this bustling hole-in-the-wall is Italy's version of fast food. But it isn't the processed, buns-full-of-sugar type outlet. It's the very best ingredients — DOP (Italian consortium quality-protected) produce and a whole lot of love.

Romans from across the city and tourists from around the world come to I Supplì to feast on its namesake — the local fried street food of choice, *supplì*. But they find a whole lot more when they arrive — in my opinion, their marinara pizza is the best in Rome! Their clients come from all walks of life: kids who pop by for an after-school snack; office workers who want a good but quick meal; working parents who have little time to cook. They leave content, and return time and time again.

The late Venanzio Sissini opened I Supplì in 1979, and in 1990 friends Loreto Bizzarri (Venanzio's brother-in-law), Giacomo Lucarelli and Enrico Bravi started working there before taking it over in 2002. They all previously worked in other industries, Loreto for instance in the banking and finance sector, but their shared love of food set them on this journey.

Loreto says, 'I Supplì started out as a small *pizzeria* and *friggitoria*, but then we started adding hot dishes like pasta — *cannelloni*, *lasagne*, eggplant (aubergine) *parmigiana*. And the rest is history!' He says the quality of their food is what gives them their competitive edge. For instance, they only use high-quality ingredients, such as San Marzano DOP tomatoes, and the same goes for their cheeses, flour, pasta and meats. 'The things we make could easily be replicated with lower-quality ingredients, but you can taste the difference, and our customers keep coming back because they're happy, so we are obviously doing something right!'

The *friggitoria* plays an important role in Roman cuisine, Loreto explains. 'Fried foods are a staple of the repertoire — from stuffed and fried zucchini (courgette) flowers and *baccalà* to double-fried Jewish-style artichokes. Every day we make the dishes that are part of the *cucina Romana*, like pasta with *coda alla vaccinara* (braised oxtail stew) or *amatriciana*. They are foods that originate from Rome, so you can't find them in any other place in the world. We maintain the traditions of the past and showcase them not only to visitors, but to Romans — younger ones especially — who have either forgotten or don't even know them.'

The focus at I Supplì has and always will be on tradition, Loreto says. 'We cook the things our mothers and grandmothers used to cook for us, that sadly will be lost if we don't continue to honour and hand them down.'

Street food as a concept is not new, and Loreto says that while initially born of necessity, it has recently evolved and improved in terms of quality. 'Society has changed and advanced. Years ago in Italy, men and children would come home at both lunch and dinner time and find a home-cooked meal on the table. This is a rarity now. Life has become more frenetic. People eat out more.' The global and more recent European economic crisis has hit Romans hard. 'They want quick and inexpensive food, but it needs to be authentic and of quality, and that's where we come in,' Loreto says.

Food customs are revered in Rome, and it's no different at I Supplì. While I'm there at least a couple of times a week, I make sure not to miss Thursdays — gnocchi day in Rome. Theirs are delicious, and I'm always astounded that for a few Euro, from a take-out joint, I can eat such a wholesome, delicious meal. Every Friday (when historically for religious reasons Italians don't eat meat), you find fried *calamari*, *baccalà* and pasta dishes with seafood.

Loreto, Enrico and Giacomo share their passion for traditional cooking with their dedicated team. This is what unites them and has been the fundamental factor in the shop's continuing success.

Salty fried *baccalà* or salt cod fillets are a staple on Roman menus, from the *trattoria* to the *pizzeria*, and of course at *friggitorie* around town. The soaking of the *baccalà* to remove excess salt and the battering process are key to this recipe by Piero Drago and Jacopo Ricci of Secondo Tradizione. They say that the *baccalà* must be soaked in water for around 48 hours, with the water changed every 8 hours or so. And to give it a crisp lightness, the batter must be ice-cold.

This version gives a nice light batter to the fish, as opposed to the heavier one often found in Rome.

FILETTI DI BACCALÀ ALLA ROMANA

(Roman-style battered salt cod)

BY PIERO DRAGO AND JACOPO RICCI, SECONDO TRADIZIONE

SERVES 4

600 g (1 lb 5 oz) baccalà (salt cod) fillets

extra virgin olive oil, for pan-frying

Batter

300 g (10½ oz/2 cups) plain (all-purpose) flour, plus extra for coating

100 g (3½ oz) cornflour (cornstarch)

2 teaspoons baking powder

1 egg yolk

300 ml (10 fl oz) light beer or lager

100 ml (3½ fl oz) sparkling water

ice cubes

Buy the *baccalà* fillets pre-soaked, or alternatively soak them in cold water for 48 hours, changing the water every 8 hours to remove the salt and rehydrate the fish.

To make the batter, mix the flour, cornflour and baking powder in a large bowl, then add the egg yolk, beer and sparkling water and whisk well to obtain a smooth batter. Do not add any salt as the *baccalà* itself is very salty.

Strain the batter through a sieve to ensure there are no lumps or sediment, then leave in the fridge for at least 1 hour to rest.

When you are ready to fry, rinse the *baccalà* fillets and dab them with paper towel to remove any moisture. Cut into strips about 2–3 cm (¾–¼ inches) thick. Pour plenty of olive oil into a large heavy-based saucepan and heat until boiling — about 170°C (340°F) on a cooking thermometer. (Test the oil with a drop of batter: as soon as it sizzles and floats about the pan, the oil is ready to go.)

Remove the batter from the fridge and add a couple of ice cubes to the mixture to ensure it stays cold.

Put a little extra flour in a bowl. Working in two or three batches, lightly coat the *baccalà* strips with flour, dip them into the batter mixture, then carefully drop into the hot oil. Fry until golden, about 4–5 minutes in total, moving them around regularly with a slotted spoon to ensure an even colour.

Drain on paper towel and serve hot.

FIORI DI ZUCCA

(Fried zucchini flowers)

BY TONI BRANCATISANO

SERVES 4

12 zucchini (courgette) flowers

125 g (4½ oz) mozzarella

6 anchovy fillets in olive oil

12 small basil leaves (optional)

100 g (3½ oz/⅔ cup) plain (all-purpose) flour

50 g (1¾ oz) cornflour (cornstarch)

25 g (1 oz) baking powder

250 ml (8½ fl oz/1 cup) ice-cold sparkling water

vegetable oil, for deep-frying

These are one of my favourite things to eat in Rome and when they are on the menu, they always end up on my plate! My local *friggitoria* sell them, and they are a popular *antipasto* at both the *pizzeria* and *trattoria*, and even at restaurants.

This version from Toni is deliciously light and crisp. Zucchini flowers are stuffed with mozzarella and some anchovy, then lightly battered and fried. I rarely ate anchovies until I moved to Rome, but now I love them. Having said that, the anchovy in this recipe does nothing more than give it a salty centre. Feel free to leave it out for a vegetarian option; Toni also adds a basil leaf to her stuffing, which is totally optional.

Remove the stamens from the centre of the zucchini flowers, leaving the flowers intact and being careful not to tear the petals.

Cut the mozzarella into 3 cm (1¼ inch) long strips and cut each anchovy in half. Place one piece of mozzarella, one piece of anchovy and one basil leaf, if using, inside each flower, closing the end by gently twisting the petals together.

Prepare the batter by mixing the flour, cornflour, baking powder and sparkling water in a bowl and whisking until smooth and lump-free.

Fill a heavy-based saucepan with vegetable oil and heat until very hot — about 200°C (400°F) on a cooking thermometer. Dip the stuffed flowers in the batter, shake off the excess, then drop them one or two at a time into the hot oil. Cook for 3–4 minutes, or until the batter is golden and crunchy, moving them around regularly with a slotted spoon to ensure an even colour.

Drain on paper towel and serve hot.

Eleonora, who gave me this recipe, says that the native Roman *mozzarella in carrozza* — 'in a carriage' — must be eaten with your hands, and that the name pays homage to the long stretchy ribbons of melted cheese, which recall the reins of horse-drawn carriages. Eleonora is Roman-American and grew up eating these fried-to-golden-perfection treats. 'Tuck into it immediately — and with your hands, remember — before it becomes gummy and loses its sinfully crisp character.'

In Rome, these are found at take-away outlets like the *friggitoria*, or on the menu at *pizzeria* as a pre-pizza snack. Often, unlike Eleonora's version, they are crumbed.

MOZZARELLA IN CARROZZA

(Mozzarella 'in a carriage')

BY ELEONORA BALDWIN

SERVES 4

400 g (14 oz) buffalo mozzarella

8 slices of white bread, crusts removed

400 g (14 oz/2⅔ cups) '00' flour or plain (all-purpose) flour, plus extra for coating

4 eggs, beaten

100 ml (3½ fl oz) cold milk

500 ml (17 fl oz/2 cups) vegetable oil, for frying

Cut the mozzarella into thin slices, then blot on paper towel to remove any excess moisture which would make the bread soggy.

Evenly distribute the mozzarella on four of the bread slices, leaving a 1 cm (½ inch) margin around the edge. Top with the remaining bread slices. Using your fingers, crimp the sandwiches around the edges to seal them into pockets, to prevent the cheese escaping.

Place the flour in a bowl. In a separate bowl, mix together the beaten eggs, milk and a good pinch of salt.

Heat the vegetable oil in a wide, heavy-based frying pan until boiling — about 180°C (350°F) on a cooking thermometer.

Coat the sandwiches with a little extra flour, then dip them into the egg mixture, making sure all the sides are covered (this can get messy). Using a spatula, carefully lower the sandwiches into the hot oil in a couple of batches and cook for 5–6 minutes, turning often, until both sides are golden and crisp.

Drain on paper towel and eat piping hot.

APERITIVO

One of my favourite pastimes and Italian traditions is the *aperitivo*. This blanket term for a pre-dinner drink — even pre-lunch for that matter — comes in a variety of formulas. And Rome is certainly not short of bars or drinking holes! Craft beer and cocktail bars seem to be the new black around town and wine is forever popular, which means visitors and locals are really spoilt for choice when it comes to not only finding a drink, but a very good one at that.

Generally, *aperitivo* time is anywhere between after work and dinner time. Dinner in Rome is never before 8pm or 9pm, and so people will have an *aperitivo* between 7pm and 9pm. It's as simple as a quick drink at the bar, to a more elaborate sit-down affair where canapés are brought to your table, or you fill a plate from a buffet selection (usually a spread of pizza, hot dishes, salads, pasta and vegetables). Really, it can be whatever you want it to be: quick, long, with one drinking partner or loads of company.

While the Milanese are said to have invented the classic *aperitivo* (with the first Campari production starting just outside the city in the early 1900s), the trend spread fast throughout Italy, and the Romans have certainly perfected it. The Aperol Spritz originates from Venice, but it's not uncommon nowadays to see a sea of the distinct orange liquid line tables and bars across Rome at *aperitivo* time.

Legend has it that until about the 1920s, pre-dinner drinks in Italy were mixed with soda water. That is until an American, Count Camilio Negroni, visited Florence and asked for gin instead — and so the Negroni (Campari, sweet vermouth and gin) was born. From here on, the *aperitivo* evolved in both sophistication and variety, with snacks added to the tables where people sipped, and mixers like *prosecco* and fruit juice added to Campari.

Paolo Dianini, the bar manager of Rome's beautiful and historic Stravinskij Bar at the luxury five-star Hotel de Russie, says *aperitivo* hour is an integral part of Italian culture and the easiest way for tourists to mix with the locals. To fit in, he says, 'Order an Aperol Spritz — it is certainly the most popular. Champagne and *Franciacorta* would be next on the list. Wine is also the classic *aperitivo* beverage and, in the warmer months, shaken cocktails like the Mojito or Caipirinha are our clients' drink of choice.'

He says that in Rome, vermouth has recently made a huge comeback. 'It's the mother of the Italian *aperitivo* and Romans love it in their drinks — especially in the classic Negroni or Americano (Campari, sweet vermouth and club soda).' Also popular, the Negroni Sbagliato ('messed-up Negroni') is made with *prosecco* instead of gin.

While the delicious signature Stravinskij Spritz — *prosecco* mixed with their 48-hour brewed house-made syrup of lemon, orange, grapefruit, passionfruit, strawberries, rhubarb and various spices including saffron — is popular with Romans and the bar's international, jet-setting crowd, my preferred cocktail is the Hugo, discovered thanks to a friend. Popular in north Italy, it has slowly (in true Italian style) made its way to Rome, and bars are increasingly starting to feature it on their drink lists. Made with *prosecco* and St-Germain (*sambuco* — not to be confused with Sambuca — and otherwise known as elderflower syrup), it's fresh for summer and a great option for those who, like me, find the Aperol Spritz too dry.

Wine is another obvious option at *aperitivo*, with a selection that leaves you anything but thirsty! Every single region in Italy produces wine. It is one of the only countries in the world that can lay claim to such a vast production and market. It also produces and sells approximately 400 million bottles of *prosecco* a year (Italy's version of Champagne — but don't ever call it that to the French or Italians!).

Not just a nation of wine drinkers as the stats suggest, beer is also very popular in Italy, and always has been. Craft beer in Rome has seen a renaissance of sorts in the last few years, and pubs and shops across the city now feature microbreweries from Italy and abroad.

Whether wine, beer or a cocktail is your drink of choice, *aperitivo* is all about winding down, having a relaxed drink and people-watching. Oh and this idea of a little snack with your drink isn't limited to the evening either. At any time of day, at any bar in Rome, if you order an alcoholic beverage it will be accompanied by some crisps or nuts or olives.

So find a bar, sit back and enjoy *la dolce vita*, Roman style.

Cin cin!

Potato croquettes are a staple Roman street food snack, and part of that delicious *fritti* (fried food) list that kicks off the *pizzeria* menu. *Crocchette* are often served as part of a mixed fried platter and are commonly seen on *aperitivo* buffets about town. Lately the old croquette has been given a little more attention, and it's not uncommon to find more gourmet varieties in Rome. At my local *friggitoria* they make a decadent four-cheese one, as well as a *baccalà* and potato version. They are super simple to make and are great as a starter to a meal or for parties, given they are the perfect finger food.

This recipe is for classic *crocchette*, but as you master the technique, try working in ingredients such as *pancetta* or different types of cheese; the combinations are endless.

CROCCHETTE DI PATATE

(Potato croquettes)

MAKES 30

2 eggs, beaten

200 g (7 oz) fine dry breadcrumbs

vegetable oil, for deep-frying

Filling

1 kg (2 lb 3 oz) floury/ boiling potatoes

2 egg yolks

pinch of freshly grated nutmeg

100 g (3½ oz) Parmigiano Reggiano, grated

To prepare the filling, rinse the whole, unpeeled potatoes and put them in a large saucepan. Cover with cold water and bring to the boil, then cook at a rapid boil for 35–40 minutes, or until just tender. Drain and leave to cool just enough to handle, then peel off the skins. While they are still warm, mash the potatoes into a purée.

In a separate bowl, beat the egg yolks with a pinch of salt and black pepper, then add to the potato purée. Season with the nutmeg and add the parmigiano. Mix well to blend the ingredients to a smooth consistency. Take a handful of mixture (around 35 g/1 oz) and form it into a cylinder shape, with the ends smoothed. Once all the *crocchette* are formed, place them on a tray lined with baking paper.

To coat the *crocchette*, put the beaten eggs in one bowl and fill another with the breadcrumbs. Dip the *crocchette* in the egg, then roll them in the breadcrumbs, using your hands to compact the coating. Place them back on the lined tray ready for frying.

Once all the *crocchette* are prepared, heat plenty of vegetable oil in a medium-sized heavy-based saucepan until boiling — about 180°C (350°F) on a cooking thermometer. Working in batches, fry three or four *crocchette* at a time in the hot oil, so the oil temperature doesn't drop too much. Cook for about 3–4 minutes, stirring with a slotted spoon to ensure they are golden all over.

Drain on paper towel and serve hot.

MOZZARELLINE FRITTE

(Fried mini-mozzarella balls)

SERVES 4

400 g (14 oz) bocconcini (fresh baby mozzarella balls), or large mozzarella balls cut into 2 cm cubes

200 g (7 oz) fine dry breadcrumbs

1 teaspoon ground cinnamon

2 eggs

1 tablespoon milk

vegetable oil, for deep-frying

Drain the mozzarella balls in a colander and pat dry with paper towel to remove any excess moisture.

In a bowl, mix the breadcrumbs with the cinnamon and season with salt and pepper. In a separate bowl, beat the eggs and milk together.

Dip each piece of mozzarella quickly in the egg mixture, then carefully roll in the breadcrumbs, patting with your hands to compact the coating.

Place the crumbed mozzarella on a tray lined with baking paper, ready for frying.

Pour plenty of vegetable oil into a large heavy-based saucepan and heat to boiling — about 170°C (340°F) on a cooking thermometer. Working in several batches, gently lower the mozzarella balls into the hot oil and fry for 2–3 minutes, stirring with a slotted spoon to ensure they are golden all over.

Drain on paper towel, before serving piping hot.

These are my guilty Roman pleasure. I find them hard to go past — I grab some at a take-away place or usually at my local *pizzeria*. Literally bocconcini of mozzarella, crumbed and fried, these morsels of salty, comfort food are easy to make at home and a huge hit at parties and with kids. While they can be prepared in advance, leave frying to the last minute and be sure to eat them hot.

In Rome these meat-stuffed, crumbed olives are known as *olive ascolane* because Romans tend to cut words and shorten everything. *Olive all'Ascolana*, as the name suggests, are from the city of Ascoli Piceno in the central Le Marche region. Apparently they were created in the 17th century by an unknown chef, who was working for a noble family. They are now a popular snack and starter all around Italy; in Rome you can grab a bag full at the *friggitoria*, or a platter of them as a starter at the *pizzeria*.

Angelo uses his aunt Elisa's recipe; she is known for her fried snacks and often fries up a batch of these to eat with a pre-dinner *aperitivo*. You can prepare these in advance, but they are best eaten freshly fried.

OLIVE ALL'ASCOLANA

(Fried stuffed olives)

BY ANGELO PREZIOSI

MAKES ABOUT 30

100 g (3½ oz/⅔ cup) plain (all-purpose) flour

1 egg, beaten

100 g (3½ oz) fine dry breadcrumbs

1 kg (2 lb 3 oz) pitted green olives

vegetable oil, for deep-frying

salt, for sprinkling

Filling

3 tablespoons extra virgin olive oil

½ onion, chopped

½ carrot, chopped

½ celery stalk, chopped

100 g (3½ oz) beef rump

100 g (3½ oz) pork loin

100 g (3½ oz) chicken breast

125 ml (4 fl oz/½ cup) dry white wine

1 egg, beaten

80 g (2¾ oz) Parmigiano Reggiano

30 g (1 oz) dry breadcrumbs

pinch of freshly grated nutmeg

juice of ½ lemon

To make the filling, heat the olive oil in a large frying pan, add the onion, carrot and celery and cook for 5 minutes over medium heat until soft, stirring now and then.

Chop the beef, pork and chicken into small pieces, then add to the pan and brown lightly for 3–4 minutes. Pour in the wine and cook for a further 10 minutes, or until the alcohol has evaporated and the liquid has reduced. Turn off the heat, leave to cool slightly, then blend the mixture in a food processor until it forms a paste.

In a bowl, combine the meat mixture with the beaten egg, parmigiano, breadcrumbs, nutmeg and lemon juice. Cover and place in the fridge to cool for at least 30 minutes.

When the filling has chilled, prepare a plate of flour, a bowl with the beaten egg and a separate plate with the breadcrumbs.

Cut each olive lengthways, all the way through. Stuff one half with the meat mixture and place the two halves back together to re-form the olive shape. Coat each one in flour, then dip in the beaten egg and roll in the breadcrumbs, patting down with your hands to compact the coating. Place the crumbed olives on a tray lined with baking paper, ready for frying.

Pour plenty of vegetable oil into a large saucepan and heat to boiling — about 170°C (340°F) on a cooking thermometer. Gradually add the olives in batches, so the oil temperature doesn't drop too much, and cook for 4–5 minutes, moving them around regularly with a slotted spoon to ensure an even golden colour.

Drain on paper towel, sprinkle with a little salt and serve hot.

ZUCCHINE IN PASTELLA

(Battered zucchini)

BY LINA PASQUALE

SERVES 4

4 medium-sized zucchini (courgettes)

salt, for sprinkling

vegetable oil, for deep-frying

Batter

300 g (10½ oz/2 cups) plain (all-purpose) flour

100 g (3½ oz) cornflour (cornstarch)

2 teaspoons baking powder

1 teaspoon salt

1 egg yolk

300 ml (10 fl oz) light beer or lager

100 ml (3½ fl oz) sparkling water

Vegetables fried in batter are my go-to snack on the run in Rome. On my way home, I often stop off at I Supplì, my local *friggitoria*, to pick up a paper bag full of fried zucchini. Don't tell anyone! They are like fries and super addictive. I love them for their saltiness and somehow convince myself that they account for some of my daily vegetable intake. I also love eating them because they remind me of my mum. This is her recipe, and while she cuts her zucchini into rounds, in Rome they are most commonly cut lengthways. This batter is versatile in that you could substitute the zucchini for any other crispy vegetable like broccoli or cauliflower. Take it from me, sage leaves come up a treat too.

Top and tail the zucchini and, leaving the skins on, cut into strips a similar size and shape as potato fries. Put them in a colander and sprinkle with salt. Leave with a heavy plate or weight on top for about 30 minutes, to drain any excess fluid and keep the zucchini crisp when frying.

Meanwhile, in a bowl, mix together the flour, cornflour, baking powder and salt. Add the egg yolk, beer and sparkling water and whisk together until the batter is smooth and free of lumps. Leave to rest for 15–20 minutes.

When you are ready to fry, heat plenty of vegetable oil in a heavy-based saucepan or deep frying pan until boiling — about 180°C (350°F) on a cooking thermometer. (Test the oil with a drop of batter: as soon as it sizzles and floats about the pan, the oil is ready to go.)

Pat the zucchini dry with paper towel, then toss a handful at a time into the batter, mixing to ensure each piece is evenly covered, before carefully lowering into the hot oil with a slotted spoon. Cook each batch until the batter is crisp and golden, about 2 minutes, turning regularly to ensure an even colour.

Drain on paper towel, sprinkle with salt and serve immediately.

MARCO LORI

Sommelier and Master of Wine

Marco Lori was born in Rome and is passionate about two things besides his family: wine and soccer. While we can't see eye to eye on the latter (he is a Lazio fan and I barrack for age-old rival, A.S. Roma), we do share a love for wine.

His curiosity for winemaking stems from his childhood when his father used to produce wine at his vineyard in south Rome. He studied agriculture at high school and went on to become a sommelier in 1995. In 2014 he became an Italian Master of Wine, of which there are only about 100 across the country, with a limited number awarded each year.

While wine intake in Rome has declined recently because of growth in the craft beer sector and a recent focus on cocktails, Marco says this is predominantly among young Romans, and wine exports have actually increased. 'Wine consumption in Italy is currently at around 35 litres per person, per annum — down from 46 litres just seven years ago. But fortunately, exports are up, in particular to the United States, where there is a growing appreciation for Italian wines. So this hasn't impacted production.'

Italy has one of the longest traditions of winemaking in the world. Marco says wine production in Rome and its surrounds began even before the Roman Empire — from the Sabine tribes to the Etruscans. Therefore, wine drinking is culturally tied to the Italian DNA, and even starts from a young age. It's not all that uncommon to see parents giving their kids a sip at the dinner table or teens being allowed to have a drop, under adult supervision. Italians don't drink wine to get drunk but to socialise and, importantly, to complement what they are eating.

On that note, Marco says that the basic principle of food and wine pairing is to match produce and wine from the same or equivalent area. For instance, Tuscan food will generally go well with Tuscan wines, or foods that grow in a warm and dry climate will go with wines produced in a similar climate. With the classics of the *cucina Romana*, he therefore suggests Lazio wines as the perfect accompaniment. 'Wines like *Frascati*, *Cesanese*, *Moscato di Terracina* or any DOC-certified labels from the Castelli Romani wine country area, *Cerveteri*, *Circeo*, *Orvieto*.'

Drinking wine throughout the course of a long Italian meal is like a journey, but there are some rules one must abide by. You generally start off the meal with an *aperitivo* (aperitif), which means *bollicine* (bubbles). Italian sparkling wine generally comes in the form of *Prosecco*, *Franciacorta* and *Trento DOC* (don't confuse these wines with Champagne of the French trademark). Then depending on how many courses, there will be some white and red, gradually moving from lighter drops to the more full-bodied.

Marco says, 'One of the major misconceptions with wine and dining is that if you start a meal with white, for instance, you must continue with it for the remainder of the meal. This couldn't be further from the truth. Where possible, wine should be matched to each dish.'

He says wine pairing is a science, but a quick and general rule of thumb can be applied. 'Go white wine with "white" foods like *carbonara*, and red with "red",

say an *amatriciana*. Sparkling wines are good with fatty or fried foods as they are structured enough to cleanse the palate. And sweet wine pairs well with dessert and contrasts perfectly with cheese.'

If it's *aperitivo* time and you don't like the classic *Prosecco*, Marco says a light, fruity and aromatic white like *Moscato*, Chardonnay, Riesling or Gewürztraminer are great choices. Rosè is another option, and if red is your preference he suggests lighter reds like Pinot Noir, *Sangiovese* or *Barbera*.

When visiting Rome, Marco says to watch out for the house wine at *trattorie* about town. 'They might be cheap, but aren't always of good quality, and a good bottle of wine won't set you back all that much in Rome anyway. Always ask for the wine list, and if there is a sommelier, ask for their tips based on what you're eating.'

Chapter
Three

ILFO

I vividly remember the first few times I went into my neighbourhood *forno* in Trastevere. It seemed that every other *signora* (older lady) and even kids got served before me. It quickly became clear to me that my inherent Australian ability to form a queue wasn't going to get me far around here. After a few visits, one of the servers told me I had to learn the Roman way — to less politely push my way to the front — which to a foreigner may seem rude or aggressive, but heck, with 60 million people living in Italy, being assertive is in the Italian DNA!

The concept of buying bread at a bakery (rather than baking it yourself at home) is said to have originated in Rome sometime around 280BC. By the time of Emperor Augustus (27BC to 14AD), there were over 250 bakeries in Rome, and even a bakers' guild. So you could say that Rome and its surrounds have a strong tradition of breadmaking.

It's not just bread you find at the *forno* in Rome. *Forno* means 'oven', and so just about anything oven-baked can be purchased, from biscuits and other sweet goods like *crostata* (a tart, commonly filled with jam or chocolate and ricotta) to pizza.

Pizza bianca and *pizza rossa* are staples on the *forno* counter, with some bakeries in the city expanding their selection to offer other types of pizza by the slice. *Pizza bianca* and *pizza rossa* translate to 'white pizza' and 'red pizza'. *Pizza bianca* is Rome's version of a flat bread or focaccia, and is fluffy, salty and addictive. *Pizza rossa* is generally *pizza bianca* but with tomato sauce atop.

Pizzette — literally little round bite-sized pizzas with tomato sauce — are also a crowd favourite at the *forno*. You will often find *porchetta* at many bakeries, which is perfect given it pairs incredibly with fresh bread for a lunch or anytime *panino* snack. *Porchetta* is rolled pork that has been seasoned with spices and baked in a wood-fired oven until it is succulent on the inside and a crispy crackling has formed on the outside. When I was a kid, my mum would prepare *porchetta* for parties, but I never ate it. I only know now what I was missing, and have done my very best to make up for lost time.

An extension of the *forno* is the *biscottificio*. *Biscotti* is the Italian blanket term for biscuits, and *biscottificio* literally means 'the biscuit shop'. I am fortunate to have one a short walk away from where I live. There is just something that speaks to the heart when you smell biscuits baking. That sweet perfume takes you back to your childhood, and for me, walking into my local, Biscottificio Innocenti, is like stepping back in time. They bake dozens and dozens of types of biscuits, and are a true neighbourhood institution.

Pizza bianca is Rome's version of a focaccia or flat bread. It's usually fluffy on the inside, with an outer crispy crunch, and a scattering of salt. You eat it with your hands and yes, your fingers should get a little oily and salty. Antico Forno Roscioli is famous for their *pizza bianca* and this is their recipe, which is not all that hard to make at home. If you want to do as the Romans do, slice a slab open and fill it with *mortadella*. In Roman dialect, this is *pizza e mortazza* and it's one of life's simple pleasures.

PIZZA BIANCA

BY ANTICO FORNO ROSCIOLI

**MAKES 2 TRAYS,
EACH ABOUT
34 x 40 CM
(13½ x 16 INCHES)**

500 g (1 lb 2 oz) strong
flour

3 teaspoons salt

1 teaspoon malt or caster
(superfine) sugar

1 teaspoon fresh yeast

50 ml (1¾ fl oz) milk

340 ml (11½ fl oz/1⅓ cups)
water

extra virgin olive oil,
for greasing

fine semolina flour,
for dusting

sea salt flakes, for
sprinkling

chopped rosemary, for
sprinkling (optional)

Sift the flour, salt and malt together into a large bowl, or the bowl of an electric stand mixer fitted with a dough hook. In a separate bowl, mix the fresh yeast into the milk, then add the water.

If you are using an electric mixer, add a little of the milk mixture into the flour, then gradually add the remaining liquid as the ingredients blend together. If you are mixing by hand, combine the liquid with the flour using a fork, then use your hands to bring the dough together. The mixture will be very soft, but if it is too wet add a little extra flour.

Once the dough is smooth, form it into a ball and place in a bowl. Rub a little olive oil over the dough, and on the underside of a sheet of plastic wrap. Cover the dough with the plastic wrap and leave to rise at room temperature overnight, or for at least 10–12 hours; in summer, leave it in a cool place.

Once the dough has risen, dust a clean surface — wooden is best — with the semolina flour. Turn the dough out and knead gently. Form into two balls and leave to rest for a further 30 minutes.

Preheat the oven to 240°C (465°F). Meanwhile, pour a little olive oil onto two baking trays, each about 34 x 40 cm (13½ x 16 inches) in size, tilting to cover the base. On the same floured surface as before, stretch each ball of dough to the same size as the trays, then drag the dough through the oil on both sides before using your fingers to press it into the tray. This will give the pizza its distinctive undulating form and maintain the pockets of air created during the long rising time.

Transfer to the oven and bake for 12–15 minutes, until the dough starts turning lightly golden.

Remove from the oven, brush the tops with more olive oil and sprinkle with sea salt and rosemary, if desired.

Enjoy hot, or leave to cool and fill with whatever ingredients you like.

PIZZA ROSSA

BY ANTICO FORNO ROSCIOLI

**MAKES 2 TRAYS,
EACH ABOUT
34 x 40 CM
(13½ x 16 INCHES)**

1 quantity Pizza Bianca
dough (see page 87)

extra virgin olive oil,
for drizzling

Sauce

400 g (14 oz) fresh
tomatoes

50 ml (1¾ fl oz) extra virgin
olive oil

1 teaspoon salt

pinch of dried **oregano**

My first memory of *pizza rossa* was as a seven-year-old in Abruzzo. We would visit the town market in the morning, and bring *pizza rossa* and bread home for lunch. I remember finding it fascinating that it was baked in one long slab and you told the server how much you wanted cut off. As in Abruzzo, this thin and tasty pizza with a simple tomato topping is found in bakeries and street stalls around Rome. This Antico Forno Roscioli version is the one they have been baking for decades, and is ever popular with Romans and tourists at their bakery. Delicious fresh out of the oven, it's also just as good cold.

Follow the instructions for the Pizza Bianca dough on page 87 and stretch it onto the baking trays, ready for the oven.

To make the sauce, peel the tomatoes by scoring a cross on the bottom of each one, put them in a heatproof bowl and cover with boiling water. Leave for 30 seconds, then move them to a bowl of cold water and remove the skins by peeling away from the cross. Cut the tomatoes in half and use a spoon to scoop out the seeds.

Use a food processor or hand-held stick blender to mix together the tomatoes, olive oil, salt and oregano until smooth.

Spread the tomato sauce over each pizza, before baking as directed on page 87.

Once cooked, drizzle with a little more olive oil before serving.

In Rome, *pizzette* can generally be bought by weight at the bakery, and are also a popular *aperitivo* snack, or served with your drink at the bar. They are puff pastry rounds with tomato sauce, which are always a hit at parties, and enjoyed by kids too. They are also a great finger food option to nibble on with a glass of wine or a cocktail. You can play around with some other topping varieties, but the classic tomato sauce version is the one that Romans have come to love. *Pizzette* can be made and baked ahead of time and frozen.

PIZZETTE

BY ANTICO FORNO ROSCIOLI

MAKES ABOUT 25

Dough

210 ml (7 fl oz) cold water

2 teaspoons salt

2 teaspoons caster
(superfine) sugar

350 g (12½ oz/2⅓ cups)
strong flour, plus extra for
dusting

Butter lamination

150 g (5½ oz/1 cup) strong
flour

250 g (9 oz) butter, at room
temperature, cut into small
chunks

Tomato sauce

250 g (9 oz) tomato passata
(puréed tomatoes)

2 tablespoons extra virgin
olive oil

pinch of dried oregano

To make the dough, pour the water into a small bowl and stir in the salt and sugar until dissolved. Put the flour in a large bowl and make a well in the centre. Pour the water mixture into the flour, mixing well with a fork from the edges, and then bringing the dough together with your hands. (You can also mix the dough using an electric stand mixer fitted with a dough hook.) Turn out the dough onto a floured surface and knead lightly until smooth and elastic. Cover the ball of dough in plastic wrap and leave to rest in the fridge for 30 minutes.

To make the butter lamination, sift the flour into a bowl, add the butter and mix until both ingredients are combined. Press between two sheets of baking paper. Rest in the fridge for at least 30 minutes.

When chilled, take the main dough from the fridge, and on a floured surface roll it out into a neat rectangle about 2 cm (¾ inch) thick. Now fold the two short sides in, to meet in the centre. Cover again with plastic wrap and place back in the fridge while you make the tomato sauce.

Put the passata, olive oil, oregano and a pinch of salt in a saucepan and heat until just beginning to boil. Remove from the heat, mix together with a hand-held stick blender until smooth, then cook over low heat for 15 minutes. Remove from the heat and leave to cool.

Place the folded-over dough back on the floured surface, then roll out the rectangle again to about a 2 cm (¾ inch) thickness. Take the butter lamination and roll it out, still between the baking paper, until it is about half the size of the dough. Place it on one half of the dough, then envelop it by folding the dough over and sealing the edges. Cover with plastic wrap and refrigerate for another 30 minutes.

Roll out the dough again and fold it in half, then roll and fold again, continuing to form layers. Repeat until the dough has been folded at least five times. If the dough starts to warm up too much, put it back in the fridge for 10 minutes before continuing.

Preheat the oven to 240°C (465°F). Line a baking tray with baking paper.

Roll out the dough to a thickness of 1 cm (½ inch). Cut out discs about 6–7 cm (2½–2¾ inches) in diameter. Place on the lined baking tray and make an indent in the centre of each one with your thumb or index finger. Place a spoonful of the cooled tomato mixture into each one.

Bake for 12–15 minutes, or until the pastry is puffed and golden. Enjoy straight from the oven, or leave to cool, as they are also good cold; Romans generally eat them cold or lukewarm.

When my mum came to Rome for the first time after I moved here, she couldn't believe her eyes when she spotted me eating *porchetta*. She'd been making it all my life, particularly for special occasions, and I'd always pass it up. I now lament all the pork I missed, because *porchetta* is truly sublime.

Porchetta is rolled, spiced pork with crackling that, put simply, just makes you happy. It is made throughout central Italy and varies slightly depending on the region. For instance, Lazio and Abruzzo share a border, but one includes garlic while the other doesn't.

PORCHETTA

(Slow-roasted pork)

BY PAOLO TOCCHIO

SERVES UP TO 12

Porchetta

2 tablespoons salt

4 rosemary sprigs, leaves picked

10 sage leaves

1 tablespoon fennel seeds

3.5 kg (7 lb 12 oz) pork belly

500 g (1 lb 2 oz) pork fillet

For cooking

250 ml (8½ fl oz/1 cup) dry white wine

250 ml (8½ fl oz/1 cup) water

4 rosemary sprigs

1 tablespoon fennel seeds

Paolo Tocchio, a butcher from Borbona in Lazio's Rieti province, shared this recipe with me, thanks to my friend Sabrina Tocchio, Paolo's cousin. The art of butchery has been in his family for generations, and in the winter time he bunkers down to make sausages, *guanciale*, *pancetta* and *prosciutto*. I love eating *porchetta* on its own, as well as the traditional Roman way — in a *panino*.

City folk flock regularly to the Castelli Romani and in particular to Ariccia, the Lazio town renowned for its *porchetta* and *fraschette*, the casual restaurants where *porchetta* and wine go hand in hand.

Create a seasoning for the *porchetta* by blitzing together the salt, rosemary, sage and fennel seeds.

Lay the pork belly on a clean work surface, skin side down, and sprinkle with a generous amount of the seasoning mix. (If you don't use it all, you can keep it to season meat or fish.)

Without cutting all the way through, slice the pork fillet down the centre lengthways, so that you can open it out like butterfly wings; you can ask your butcher to do this, if you prefer. Place the pork fillet on top of the pork belly, then roll it up, with the pork fillet inside, as tightly as possible. Tie tightly at regular intervals with kitchen string. Pierce the skin with a knife over the entire surface.

Wrap the entire *porchetta* in foil and allow to rest in the fridge overnight, or for at least 6 hours.

Preheat the oven to 220°C (430°F). Add the wine, water, rosemary sprigs and fennel seeds to a roasting tray (or a baking dish) with a roasting rack on top.

Place the *porchetta*, still covered in foil, on the rack part of the tray, so that as the liquid evaporates during cooking it will help to keep the *porchetta* moist.

Bake for 1 hour, then take the *porchetta* out of the oven and remove the foil. Place the meat back in the oven.

Reduce the oven temperature to 200°C (400°F) and bake for a further 3 hours (calculate 1 hour of cooking time for every 1 kg/ 2 lb 3 oz of meat). If the liquid dries out, top up with more water or wine, and turn the pork every 30 minutes to ensure the skin becomes crispy and 'crackles'.

Remove from the oven and allow to rest before carving.

I love the name for these *biscotti* because it's so literal and real: 'ugly but good'. And that's because they are indeed delicious and addictive, but nothing much to look at — and yet displayed at cake shops and bakeries across Rome and Lazio. An Italian meringue of sorts, these are easy to make and are crispy on the outside, with a soft and chewy centre. *Brutti ma buoni* are the truly perfect reminder not to judge a book by its cover.

BRUTTI MA BUONI

(Ugly but good biscuits)

MAKES 30

100 g (3½ oz) shelled hazelnuts

60 g (2 oz) blanched almonds

2 egg whites

lemon juice

140 g (5 oz) icing (confectioners') sugar

Preheat the oven to 170°C (340°F). Place the hazelnuts on a baking tray and toast them for 2–3 minutes. Leave to cool, then roughly chop or blend them, together with the almonds.

Using an electric mixer, whisk the egg whites with a few drops of lemon juice. When the egg whites begin to thicken, gradually add the icing sugar and continue to whisk until they form a stiff foam that stands up in peaks.

Gently fold in the hazelnuts and almonds with a spoon, being careful not to knock the air out of the egg whites.

When the nuts are evenly distributed, place the mixture in a heavy-based saucepan over medium heat and continue to stir gently with a wooden spoon. When the mixture starts to come away easily from the base and side of the pan, remove from the heat.

Using two tablespoons, shape the mixture into balls and place on a baking tray lined with baking paper, leaving a little space in between to allow for spreading.

Bake at 160°C (320°F) for 20 minutes, then leave to cool. The biscotti are best enjoyed straight away, but will keep for up to 1 week in an airtight container.

CROSTATA DI MARMELLATA

(Jam tart)

BY TONI BRANCATISANO

SERVES 8

250 g (9 oz/1⅔ cups) '00' flour

100 g (3½ oz) caster (superfine) sugar

110 g (4 oz) butter

2–3 tablespoons chilled water

500 g (1 lb 2 oz) jam

In a food processor mix together the flour, sugar, butter and a pinch of salt until the mixture resembles breadcrumbs.

While the food processor is still running, add the chilled water and continue to mix until the mixture begins to form large clumps, stopping the machine before the mixture forms a ball.

Turn the pastry out on to a lightly floured surface and knead gently to bring together. Divide the pastry into two parts, one larger than the other.

Form the larger part into a disc and cover in plastic wrap then roll out the smaller part between two pieces of baking paper, refrigerating both parts, preferably overnight, or for at least 2 hours.

Preheat the oven to 180°C (350°F).

Remove the larger disc of pastry from the fridge and roll it out to fit the base of a 22 cm (8¾ inch) round tart tin. Use it to line the base of the tin, cutting off any excess. Fill the tart with your jam of choice, then use the smaller piece of rolled-out pastry to cut out strips to criss-cross over the top of the jam.

Bake for 45 minutes, or until the pastry is golden. Allow to cool before cutting into slices with a sharp knife.

A *crostata* is an Italian-style jam tart that Italians enjoy at any time of day, starting from breakfast. When I tasted this one by my friend Toni, I knew I had to share it. In Rome you can buy a slice or an entire *crostata* at the bakery, and it is commonly on the *trattoria* dessert list. It's a great dessert option if you're looking to create something sweet and substantial, as opposed to your rich and creamy desserts. Toni says it is one of those really easy sweets that takes no time (or much skill) to make, and is always lovely to have on hand in the kitchen, best enjoyed with a tea or coffee or with some good-quality vanilla *gelato*.

STEFANIA INNOCENTI

Biscottificio Innocenti

The term *biscottificio* literally means 'biscuit shop' or factory, and while over the last few decades the role of the biscuit maker has all but been absorbed into the *forno* (bakery) or the *pasticceria* (cake shop), quite a few still exist around Italy. But there are few as special in Rome as Biscottificio Innocenti in my neighbourhood Trastevere.

On one of the picturesque streets the neighbourhood is famous for, the perfume of freshly baked *biscotti* lures you in way before you even see the shop. When you walk through the door, it's a feast for the eyes and your inner child. Aesthetically, the place has not changed one bit since Stefania Innocenti's grandfather opened it in the 1940s. As a third-generation biscuit maker, she says the art is in her DNA.

'It comes naturally to me because it's what I've always done. We never sell a product without having first tasted and loved it ourselves.'

Stefania says the heart of the shop is the 16-metre-long (52½ feet) oven, which her family purchased in the 1960s. There are always trays of multiple biscuit varieties coming out of the oven or stacked up on top of it; that grand oven is the centrepiece of this family tradition that sees them continuing to bake over 60 types of biscuits and sweet treats daily.

During the Second World War, Stefania's grandfather produced biscuits in large quantities as rations for soldiers. Her parents eventually took over, and the production changed slightly to start incorporating different ingredients. They began baking smaller quantities, but introduced new

varieties. Stefania says they continue to honour traditional recipes, the ones that are appreciated and revered by their customers, but mix in more and more new shapes and flavours as time goes on. The one constant is that every single *biscotto*, pastry or tart is handmade. They are also committed to using only the best-quality ingredients, and never use preservatives.

When I first stumbled upon this gem, I couldn't believe my eyes. The nostalgia of seeing generational businesses even in a country like Italy, where they are much more common, makes you smile. And when the *biscotti* taste as good as Stefania's, all the more so. But sometimes I don't even pop in to buy anything (not that she ever lets me leave without tasting a biscuit or giving me a little something to take home); I stop by to feel Stefania's warmth. The Innocenti family treat you like their own. In the

early days, when she hadn't even met my family yet, but, knowing that I lived so far from home, she would often ask me if I'd heard from them or how they were doing.

When I do stop to buy some biscuits it's always something chocolate-coated, and anything with jam. Their *brutti ma buoni* ('ugly but good', chocolate and hazelnut biscuits, page 97) are also divine. Stefania and I have a chat; her generosity of spirit makes my day and she wraps my biscuits in the Innocenti signature wrapping. Customers walk in and out, locals and tourists alike, and they each walk out with biscuits in hand and a smile.

When asked what customers love about the *biscottificio*, Stefania says, 'When they walk in, they feel our strong sense of family and taste the traditions that remain unchanged. So many say they feel like they've stepped back in time.'

> "When they walk in, they feel our strong sense of family and taste the traditions that remain unchanged. So many say that they feel like they've stepped back in time."

STEFANIA INNOCENTI,
BISCOTTIFICIO INNOCENTI

A sweet, simple pleasure, this ricotta and black cherry (or sour cherry) tart has its origins in Rome's Jewish Ghetto, but is now a crowd-pleaser on *trattoria* menus across the city. One of the best places to try it in Rome is at Boccione, the famous Jewish bakery in Via del Portico d'Ottavia, because theirs is said to be the original recipe, dating back to the 18th century when papal law banned Jews from trading dairy products. The *crostata* became a loophole for bakers who began hiding *ricotta* between layers of pastry and cherries.

Boccione didn't share the recipe with me because it has never left their premises. But Toni's version honours the classic and is testament to her excellent baking skills. She is a *crostata* queen and hers is just how it should be: crumbly crust, lush jam and lighty sweetened *ricotta*.

CROSTATA DI RICOTTA E VISCIOLE

(Ricotta and sour cherry tart)

BY TONI BRANCATISANO

SERVES 8–10

1 egg yolk

1 tablespoon milk

icing (confectioners') sugar, for dusting

PASTRY

300 g (10½ oz/2 cups) plain (all-purpose) flour, plus extra for dusting

150 g (5½ oz) cold butter

150 g (5½ oz) sugar

2 eggs, plus 1 egg yolk

zest of 1 lemon

FILLING

300 g (10½ oz) jar of sour cherry jam

400 g (14 oz) sheep's milk ricotta

80 g (2¾ oz) sugar

2 eggs

1 tablespoon Sambuca

To make the pastry, add all the ingredients to a food processor and mix until a dough forms. Turn out onto a lightly floured surface, knead a little and form into a flat disc, adding a little extra flour if the dough is sticky. Cover with plastic wrap and refrigerate for at least 30 minutes.

Preheat the oven to 170°C (340°F).

Roll out the pastry and use it to line a 24 cm (9½ inch) tart tin, reserving the leftover dough to make a lattice topping. Prick the base of the pastry with a fork, but don't trim the pastry edge just yet.

Spoon the cherry jam into the tart tin, smoothing it evenly over the pastry.

In a bowl, mix together the ricotta, sugar, eggs and Sambuca until well combined. Gently spoon the ricotta mixture on top of the jam.

Roll out the reserved pastry, cut it into even strips, and lay them in a criss-cross fashion on top of the filling. Press the pastry ends into the pastry border, then use a sharp knife to trim away all the overlapping pastry.

Lightly beat together the egg yolk and milk, then brush it over the pastry strips and border with a pastry brush.

Bake for about 50 minutes, or until the pastry is lightly golden and the ricotta has set.

Remove from the oven, allow to cool, and dust with icing sugar before serving.

✳ **NOTE:** Instead of jam, it is common to make this *crostata* with fresh black cherries.

CIAMBELLINE AL VINO

(Sweet wine biscuits)

BY VIVIANA GORI

MAKES 30

500 g (1 lb 2 oz/3⅓ cups) plain (all-purpose) flour

2 teaspoons baking powder

150 g (5½ oz) sugar, plus extra for coating

125 ml (4 fl oz/½ cup) sunflower oil

125 ml (4 fl oz/½ cup) red wine

2 tablespoons unsweetened cocoa powder

100 ml (3½ fl oz) Sambuca

I asked my beautiful Roman-born friend Viviana for the recipe to these simple and delicious ring-shaped biscuits. Light, crunchy and rustic, this version includes cocoa for a sweet yet bitter hit. The main ingredient, as the name suggests, is wine, and it is also customary to serve these biscuits with red wine for dipping. Found all around Rome, they are especially common in the Lazio countryside, the Castelli Romani. Traditionally peasant or working-class food, they are cheap and easy to make, and will keep for days in an airtight container.

Preheat the oven to 180°C (350°F).

Sift the flour, baking powder, sugar and a pinch of salt together into a large bowl and make a well in the centre. Add the sunflower oil, wine, cocoa and Sambuca into the centre of the well. Begin to mix carefully with a fork, moving the dry ingredients into the centre of the well.

Once mixed, turn the mixture onto a clean floured surface and use your hands to form it into a soft, smooth, slightly sticky dough.

Working on a clean but unfloured surface, so that the dough rolls into 'snakes' easily, divide the dough into smaller pieces, then roll each one into a sausage shape about 1 cm (½ inch) in diameter.

Cut into 15–20 cm (6–8 inch) lengths and shape into rings, pressing down slightly on the ends to form a doughnut shape.

Dip one side of each ring into a bowl of extra sugar, placing them on a baking tray lined with baking paper.

Bake for 20 minutes, then remove from the oven and leave to cool, before dunking in sweet wine, milk or tea.

Panettone is Italy's version of the traditional English Christmas fruit cake. I was never a huge fan of *panettone* growing up in Australia, as the majority of the ones you find are processed and store-bought. When I moved to Italy, I noticed that during the festive season, many people bought their *panettone* at the *forno* or *pasticceria,* and being able to eat a freshly made one was what eventually convinced me that *panettone* is actually enjoyable. My friend Toni makes these super-cute mini individual ones, which are sure to become a Christmas favourite in your home too.

MINI PANETTONE

BY TONI BRANCATISANO

MAKES 10

200 g (7 oz) sultanas
(golden raisins)

125 ml (4 fl oz/½ cup) rum

3 teaspoons brewer's yeast

330 ml (11 fl oz) lukewarm
water

60 g (2 oz) caster
(superfine) sugar

60 g (2 oz/⅓ cup) brown
sugar

700 g (1 lb 9 oz/4⅔ cups)
'00' flour

3 eggs

175 g (6 oz) soft butter,
melted but not hot, plus
extra melted butter for
glazing

olive oil, for greasing

finely grated zest of
2 oranges

110 g (4 oz) mixed candied
citrus peels, chopped

Soak the sultanas in the rum for 20–30 minutes, then drain and set aside; reserve the rum for another use.

Combine the yeast, water and sugars in a bowl and allow to stand for 10 minutes, or until foamy.

Using an electric stand mixer fitted with a dough hook, mix the flour and eggs until combined. Slowly incorporate the yeast mixture until a dough forms. With the mixer running, slowly add the melted butter and continue kneading until well combined. The dough should be smooth, soft and slightly sticky. If it appears too wet, add a little more flour.

Place the dough in a large oiled bowl, cover with a clean dry tea towel and leave to prove in a warm place for about 1 hour, or until it has doubled in size.

Knock back the dough by giving it a few punches to remove any air bubbles. Sprinkle over the rum-soaked sultanas, orange zest and mixed peel. On a lightly floured work surface, knead the fruit into the dough. Continue to knead for 5–10 minutes, adding more flour as necessary, until the dough is soft and pliable, but not sticky.

Form the dough into a smooth ball, then divide into 10 balls of equal weight (about 130 g/4½ oz each). Place each one in an 8 cm (3¼ inch) *panettone* paper casing on a baking tray. Cover loosely with plastic wrap and leave to rise again for 1 hour in a warm place.

Meanwhile, preheat the oven to 200°C (400°F).

Bake the *panettone* for 10 minutes, then reduce the oven temperature to 180°C (350°F) and bake for a further 10 minutes.

Reduce the heat again to 160°C (320°F) and bake for another 20 minutes, or until the tops are well browned, and a skewer inserted into a *panettone* comes out clean.

Remove from the oven, brush the tops with a little melted butter and leave to cool on a wire rack.

The *panettone* are best enjoyed fresh, but can be stored for up to 1 week in an airtight container.

THE NEW ROMANS

New dining concepts and trends

While the culinary DNA of Rome is steeped in history and tradition, the city is still a modern capital that evolves constantly with new concepts and influences. Whether it be a famous chef who regularly brings back the tastes and techniques of their travels or the young Romans trying to break through with innovative ideas, there is always something new on the Roman dining scene, and some of these are even making waves around the world. For instance, renowned Roman pizza maker, Stefano Callegari, has just brought his *trapizzino* (the now famous gourmet pizza pocket) to the United States, Japan and Australia. These modern-day Romans are making headlines and setting new trends.

CLASSICS ON THE RUN

Italians have never been strangers to the *panino* (a breadroll sandwich), but the Roman landscape has started to see new ways of presenting them. One of my favourite stalls at the Testaccio Market is Mordi e Vai ('bite and run'). Owner Sergio Esposito is a retired butcher, so the meats here are prime quality. The stall has been so successful because the formula is so simple. You choose a dish, from crumbed meat cutlets to *l'allesso* (succulent boiled meat) for the tame, or the full Roman offal selection (tripe; tongue; *coratella* — heart, lungs and liver) for the adventurous, and Sergio fills your *panino*, sometimes soaking the bread in the tasty, lard-filled oil used to cook the dishes. Testaccio Market has become a haven for gastronomes with food outlets popping up throughout, but the *panini* at Mordi e Vai are so mouthwatering, you'll not want to try anything else.

THE SPEAKEASY

The first speakeasy on Rome's bar scene opened in 2010. Before that, Romans had never been exposed to the underground cocktail scene that seems to have taken the rest of the world by storm. These hipster bars are quietly popping up all over town, found in butcher shops, barbers and garages.

The Jerry Thomas Project is located in a dark alleyway with no other bars or restaurants, right by Piazza Navona. As you walk down the street, you would never suspect that one of Rome's best cocktail bars lies therein. To get into the bar you must book ahead and provide a password at the door, and owner Alessandro Procoli says they don't make exceptions for anyone. He and his business partner Leonardo Leuci travelled the world and researched extensively to give this project life. Alessandro says the philosophy of their speakeasy is to showcase the mixology of years gone by. 'Here in Rome, we gave birth to the first speakeasy of its kind in Italy, and we are still the benchmark, inspiration and role model for bars and mixologists across the country.'

GOURMET GELATO

Gelato is serious business in Italy. And while many *gelaterie* in Rome claim to produce homemade, artisanal *gelato*, the truth is, many don't.

In the early 2000s, Maria Agnese Spagnuolo moved to Rome from Puglia in Italy's south to pursue her theatre career. When she was diagnosed as a coeliac, she walked away from the arts world and began nurturing her childhood passion — *gelato*! And so Fatamorgana was born. With multiple locations across the city, overseas expansion is on the cards too.

I'm not talking about just any *gelato*. Fatamorgana *gelato* is 100% natural, homemade and gluten-free (even the cones). They are completely free of artificial colouring or additives, with lactose-free and vegan varieties also available.

The flavours you find here aren't necessarily the ones Italians were raised on. While they produce all the classics (lemon, pistachio, strawberry...), they've become famous for unique flavour combinations, such as Kentucky tobacco-infused chocolate; basil, pear and Gorgonzola; rose petal and black rice — and whatever else is in season. Maria Agnese says, 'The secret to our success has been our ability to recognise and select prize produce — from varying types of almonds and pistachios, to quality fruits.'

Vittorio Olivieri works at my local Fatamorgana in Trastevere. He always serves my *gelato* or makes my frappe with a smile. This young Roman, who also lives in the neighbourhood, loves his job.

'When I walk through the neighbourhood,' he says, 'people recognise me and even offer to shout me a coffee at the local bar. I might not know their name, but I know what their favourite *gelato* flavour is!'

Chapter Four

IL MER

CATO

The market in Italy is not just about buying food. It's a true cultural experience linked to the Italian way of life. It's here that you build relationships with the stall-holders, fishmongers and cashiers. They often know your name, where you live, and definitely what you're cooking.

I have a local market around the corner from where I live. The fresh food market in Piazza di San Cosimato is small, but has everything from fruit and vegetables, cheese and *salumi*, to seafood and meat. At any market in Rome, it doesn't matter how many fruit and vegetable stalls there are, locals always have 'their' *fruttivendolo* (fruit and vegetable seller).

Mine are Pietro and Concetta. When I get to their stall, it's not just the warm welcome that makes me happy, but their stories, and their interest in mine. Concetta says she was practically born at the market because her mother went into labour here. Her parents owned the stall and, shortly after she came into the world, she lay in her basket right by the crates of produce — so knowing how to select the best fruit and vegetables is in her very being. In the colder months, Pietro is often seen peeling artichokes, and is always happy to demonstrate the right way to prepare them to passers-by.

The market is at the heart of Italian cooking because the diet is constructed on the seasonality of produce. You will not find summer vegetables on the menu in winter. It's rare to find them even in a supermarket. For instance, artichokes — king in Rome — can only be found out of season on a *trattoria* menu if they are imported. This is not very common, but some restaurants catering to tourists want to showcase Roman food all year round.

In Rome, I don't watch the calendar to keep an eye on when winter or spring is coming — I can tell by the selection at my market stand, and just by looking at the colours. The vibrant reds, yellows and pinks of summer start to make way for the warmer browns and oranges of autumn. I know that winter has just about started when I see *puntarelle* on menus across the city. This particular variety of chicory (also known as *catalogna* or asparagus chicory) has a pleasantly bitter taste and is prepared as a deliciously crisp salad with an olive oil, garlic, vinegar and anchovy dressing. I love eating it, but also love seeing buckets of iced water at the market as the *puntarelle* are shaved and left to soak so that they curl up.

Whenever you're in Rome, make sure you visit one of the fresh food markets. Some of the best (and easiest to access from the city centre) include: San Cosimato Market (Trastevere), Testaccio Market (Testaccio), San Giovanni di Dio Market (Monteverde) and Trionfale Market (Prati).

It's one of the most authentic things to do in the city, and will give you a real taste of local life. The sights, sounds and smells will stay with you long after your Roman holiday has ended.

PUNTARELLE

BY ANGELO PREZIOSI

SERVES 4

500 g (1 lb 2 oz) puntarelle (Catalogna chicory), trimmed

90 ml (3 fl oz) extra virgin olive oil

2 tablespoons white wine vinegar

2 garlic cloves, finely chopped

8 anchovy fillets in olive oil

The first sign of winter in Rome is seeing *puntarelle* chalked up on blackboard menus in *trattorie* across town. And if they're not written on the menu anywhere, nine times out of ten just ask and you shall receive. Angelo's recipe follows the classic way for dressing these local Roman crisp, slightly bitter greens, which are part of the endive family. In Rome you can buy them at the market or supermarket already prepared, but for those who enjoy a challenge, you can shave them with a *tagliapuntarelle* (a special wooden gadget) to have them curl as they should.

When *puntarelle* aren't in season or you can't get your hands on them, Angelo says the salty anchovy vinaigrette also goes well with lamb's lettuce (known in Italy as *valeriana* or *songino*) or baby spinach leaves.

If preparing the *puntarelle* yourself, remove the leaves and cut the light green stems lengthways into strips using a sharp knife or a *tagliapuntarelle*. Add the strips to ice-cold water and leave for 5–10 minutes, until they curl up and turn crispy. Drain well.

To make the dressing, pour the olive oil into a bowl and add the vinegar, garlic and anchovies. Mix with a whisk or a fork until the liquid has emulsified, leaving a few large pieces of anchovy intact. Taste and season with a little salt if necessary.

Toss the drained *puntarelle* in the dressing and serve immediately. In Rome they are generally enjoyed as a side dish.

CICORIA RIPASSATA

(Sautéed chicory)

BY ANGELO PREZIOSI

SERVES 4

1 kg (2 lb 3 oz) wild chicory, trimmed

60 ml (2 fl oz/¼ cup) extra virgin olive oil

1 garlic clove, finely sliced

2 red chillies, seeded and finely chopped

In Italy, when you order meat or fish, *un secondo*, it almost always comes on its own without a side. You order your side dishes, *contorni*, separately. Anything *ripassata in padella* is a seasonal vegetable that is usually sautéed in a pan with olive oil, garlic and a hint of hot chilli. If you can't find chicory or dandelion greens, this works just as well with spinach or silverbeet (Swiss chard). This is Angelo's recipe and he says to enjoy the leftovers the next day in a sandwich!

Bring a large saucepan of salted water to the boil. Rinse the chicory and add to the pan. Blanch for 5 minutes, ensuring the stalks remain firm.

Drain the chicory and rinse it under cold water to maintain its bright green colour. Squeeze the moisture out using your hands.

In a frying pan, heat the olive oil, together with the garlic and chilli. Cook gently over low heat for 2 minutes to flavour the oil.

Add the chicory and cook for 5 minutes, mixing well to coat the leaves with the oil. Season with salt.

Serve hot or cold.

BROCCOLO ROMANESCO

(Roman broccoli)

BY ANGELO PREZIOSI

SERVES 4

1 Romanesco broccoli

60 ml (2 fl oz/¼ cup) extra virgin olive oil

2 garlic cloves, finely sliced

1 red chilli, seeded and chopped

3 anchovy fillets in olive oil

Roman-style broccoli is bright green and almost cauliflower-looking. With this popular Roman side dish, Angelo says you could also use it as a base to create one of my favourite pasta dishes, *pasta e broccoli* — just toss your cooked pasta in the pan with a splash of olive oil or pasta water to give it a little sauce. This popular style of cooking vegetables works with many other vegetables and greens, such as regular broccoli, or cauliflower.

Bring a large saucepan of salted water to the boil. Cut the broccoli into florets and cook for about 10 minutes, until just tender.

Meanwhile, heat the olive oil in a frying pan, add the garlic and chilli and gently cook over low heat for 2–3 minutes to infuse the oil, being careful not to burn the garlic. Add the anchovies and continue to cook until they dissolve in the oil.

Drain the broccoli and add to the pan, stirring well. Cook together for 5 minutes, or until the broccoli is soft and coated with the infused oil. Serve warm.

CARCIOFI ALLA ROMANA

(Roman-style artichokes)

BY GINA TRINGALI

SERVES 4

1 lemon

8 Romanesco or globe artichokes

1 small bunch wild mint or calamint

3 garlic cloves

360 ml (12 fl oz) water or dry white wine

3 tablespoons extra virgin olive oil

Gina Tringali is a successful Italian-American food and travel writer based in Rome, and is co-owner of tour operator Casa Mia Italy Food & Wine. She shared this recipe with me and tells me that when *Romanesco* or *mammole* artichokes (similar to the globe variety) are in season, she could eat them every day. This purple and green variety are available in Rome from February to May. Fresh, simple and healthy, *carciofi alla Romana* are stuffed with garlic and *mentuccia* (a wild Roman mint, often referred to as lesser calamint), and cooked gently, with their stalks upwards, in water and olive oil until they are fragrant and tender. Gina says the key to this dish is prepping the artichokes well. The tough outer leaves are cut away, leaving a rose-like flower. Remember that artichokes oxidise quickly and can turn brown, so keep them in your lemon water until they are ready to be seasoned.

Fill a bowl with water, squeeze in the juice from the lemon, add the lemon rind and stir.

Trim the artichokes by cutting off the top quarter of the head and removing the tough outer leaves. Trim the stems, leaving about 5–7 cm (2–2¾ inches) attached. Trim the outer layer of the stems and remove the centre, using a spoon to scoop out the hairy choke. Once cleaned, immediately place the artichokes in the lemon water to stop them turning black.

Finely chop the mint and garlic, and season with salt and freshly ground black pepper. Drain the artichokes well and fill the centre of each artichoke with the mint mixture.

Stand the artichokes, stem side up, in a heavy-based saucepan wide enough to hold them all in one layer. Pour in the water or wine and drizzle with the olive oil.

Cover and cook over medium–low heat for about 1 hour, or until tender. Test if the artichokes are ready by pushing a toothpick into the base of the stem.

Serve warm, or at room temperature.

MARKET GUIDE

Seasonality in Italy is not just about the fruits and vegetables in season, but seafood too. The Mediterranean alone boasts almost 40 fish species and, while nowadays seafood varieties are generally available all year round, Italian fishmongers say the ones that are seasonal are those that are in the stage before or after their reproductive phase. So ask your fishmonger what's in season to ensure you're getting your fish at its very best.

While in most supermarkets you can find particular produce all year round, keep this seasonal guide in mind as you shop. The produce that is in season is really what will shine on your plate.

WINTER

Vegetables

artichoke, beetroot (beet), broccoli, brussels sprouts, cabbage, cardoon or artichoke thistle, carrot, cauliflower, celery, chicory, endive, fennel, Jerusalem artichoke, leek, lettuce, mushrooms, onion, potato, radicchio, red cabbage, silverbeet (Swiss chard), spinach, turnip tips or broccoli rabe, turnip, white cabbage

Fruit & nuts

almonds, apples, clementines, grapefruit, lemons, mandarins, oranges, pears, persimmons, pineapple, pomegranate

Fish

cod, hake, mullet, sardine, sea bass, sole

SPRING

Vegetables

artichoke, asparagus, beans, beetroot (beet), carrot, broad beans, broccoli, brussels sprouts, cauliflower, celery, cucumber, dandelion, endive, fava (broad) beans, fennel, horseradish, leek, lettuce, onion, peas, potato, radicchio, radish, rhubarb, spinach, spring onion (scallion), tomato, turnip, zucchini (courgette)

Fruit & nuts

apples, apricots, blood orange, cherries, grapefruit, kiwi fruit, lemons, loquat, mandarins, oranges, peaches, pears, strawberries

Fish

anchovies, cod, hake, mackerel, mullet, red mullet, sardines, sea bass, snapper, sole, swordfish, tuna

SUMMER

Vegetables

asparagus, basil, beans, beetroot (beet), cabbage, capsicum (bell pepper), carrot, celery, cucumber, eggplant (aubergine), fava (broad) beans, lettuce, onion, peas, potato, radish, rocket (arugula), silverbeet (Swiss chard), spinach, tomatoes, zucchini (courgette)

Fruit & nuts

apricots, blackberries, blueberries, cherries, figs, peaches, plums, raspberries, rockmelon (netted melon/cantaloupe), strawberries, watermelon, wild strawberries

Fish

anchovies, bream, cod, hake, mackerel, mullet, red mullet, sardines, sea bass, snapper, sole, swordfish, tuna

AUTUMN

Vegetables

beans, beetroot (beet), broccoli, brussels sprouts, capsicum (bell pepper), cardoon or artichoke thistle, carrot, cauliflower, celery, chicory, eggplant (aubergine), fennel, leek, lettuce, mushrooms, potato, pumpkin (winter squash), shallots, silverbeet (Swiss chard), spinach, spring onion (scallion), tomatoes, turnip tips or broccoli rabe, zucchini (courgette)

Fruit & nuts

chestnuts, figs, grapes, hazelnuts, lemons, mandarins, oranges, pears, persimmons, pomegranate, quince, rockmelon (netted melon/cantaloupe), walnuts

Fish

anchovies, bream, cod, hake, mackerel, mullet, red mullet, sardines, sea bass, snapper, sole, swordfish, tuna

ALICIOTTI CON L'INDIVIA

(Anchovy and endive bake)

BY LAURA RAVAIOLI

SERVES 4–6

1.5 kg (3 lb 5 oz) curly endive (chicory)

800 g (1 lb 12 oz) fresh anchovies

100 ml (3½ fl oz) extra virgin olive oil

1 garlic clove, finely chopped

small bunch of Italian (flat-leaf) parsley, roughly chopped

Clean the endive by removing the stalks and the hard outer leaves. Take the white interior leaves and rinse them under running water. Pat dry with a clean tea towel and roughly chop. Sprinkle with salt and leave in a colander for a few hours to drain away any excess water.

Preheat the oven to 180°C (350°F).

If the anchovies need to be cleaned and filleted, start by removing the head and cutting lengthways down the belly, leaving the back attached. Remove the bones and interiors and open each one out like a butterfly. Rinse the cleaned anchovies and place on paper towel to dry.

Pour about half the olive oil into a 24 cm (9½ inch) circular baking tin or dish (one that is not too heavy). Spread half the endive leaves across the base. Place the anchovies on top in an even layer, season with a pinch of salt and freshly ground black pepper and sprinkle with the garlic and parsley. Cover with the rest of the endive and drizzle with the remaining olive oil.

Bake for 40 minutes. Serve at room temperature, or slightly warm.

History tells us that this dish of baked fresh anchovies and endive was invented by Roman Jews in the Ghetto, in response to a 17th century ban that prohibited Jews from combining dark-fleshed fish with salad leaves. Romans love their anchovies, and they are especially popular in Roman-Jewish cuisine. Famous Roman-Jewish TV chef Laura Ravaioli shared this dish with me, and I only got to know it since living in Rome. It's easy to prepare, especially if you ask your fishmonger to fillet and butterfly your anchovies for you.

Served as a main course or appetiser, it's also a great sharing dish, the bitter hit of endive perfectly balancing the light and delicate flavour of fresh anchovies.

LA CONCIA

(Fried, marinated zucchini)

BY LAURA RAVAIOLI

SERVES 4–6

2 kg (4 lb 6 oz) Roman
zucchini (courgette), or
regular zucchini (see Note)

50 ml (1¾ fl oz) kosher
wine vinegar or white wine
vinegar

4 garlic cloves, peeled

10 basil leaves, roughly
chopped

vegetable oil, for
deep-frying

salt, for sprinkling

100 ml (3½ fl oz) extra
virgin olive oil

Top and tail each zucchini, then cut them lengthways into slices about 2–3 mm thick. Pat away any excess moisture with paper towel and leave on a clean tea towel (dish towel) to dry overnight, or for at least 12 hours. Meanwhile, pour the vinegar into a small bowl, add the garlic and basil and also leave to infuse overnight.

When you are ready to cook the zucchini, heat plenty of vegetable oil in a large heavy-based saucepan until boiling — about 170°C (340°F) on a cooking thermometer. Working in batches, deep-fry the zucchini for a couple of minutes, or until golden.

Drain with a slotted spoon and place in layers in a glass dish or bowl, lightly sprinkling each layer with salt.

Pour the infused vinegar mixture over the zucchini, then drizzle with the olive oil. Leave to cool, then cover and place in the fridge, stirring occasionally to allow the zucchini to absorb the flavours.

Serve cold the next day.

✳ NOTE: Roman zucchini are lighter in colour than regular zucchini and, when sold in Rome, often have the flower still attached to the end. They are great for frying, because they have a lower water content, and so retain less water during cooking. They are difficult to obtain outside Italy, but regular zucchini should also work fine here.

This easy-to-make vegetable dish, popular in Roman-Jewish cuisine, was given to me by Laura, who has made a wonderful career from her passion for sharing Roman-Jewish cuisine with the world. *La concia* is basically fried zucchini, marinated in vinegar and served with fresh mint or basil, and is absolutely delicious. Laura cuts her zucchini lengthways, but often you will see them cut into rounds — the choice is yours! As with many Jewish dishes, you can eat this a day or two after you prepare it; traditionally it was prepared in advance to eat on the Sabbath, when Jews weren't allowed to cook or work. While *la concia* is specific to the Roman-Jewish ghetto and may have originated in Rome, it is likely that it was first made by Spanish Jews who fled to Italy after the Spanish Inquisition in the late 15th century. It is also similar to the Neapolitan *zucchini alla scapace*.

Piero Drago and Jacopo Ricci gave me this recipe as a really versatile side dish. It's a great accompaniment to meat or any main meal, but substantial enough to sit on its own for lunch or dinner. They use *broccolo Romanesco*, but you can use any kind of broccoli, or even cauliflower.

Even though it is called a *torta*, it is not a 'cake' of course — *torta* being a blanket Italian term for anything that has been formed or has a shape; essentially it is like a bake or a smash of sorts. The garlic and chilli give so much flavour; the best way to enhance the dish is with a slug of good extra virgin olive oil.

TORTA DI PATATE E BROCCOLI ROMANI

(Roman broccoli and potato smash)

BY PIERO DRAGO AND JACOPO RICCI, SECONDO TRADIZIONE

SERVES 4

2 large waxy/boiling potatoes

1 Romanesco broccoli

60 ml (2 fl oz/¼ cup) extra virgin olive oil

1 garlic clove, finely chopped

1 red chilli, seeded and finely chopped

Boil the potatoes with their skins on in a saucepan of salted water for about 30 minutes, or until tender. Drain, and when cool enough to handle, peel off the skins and cut the potatoes into large pieces.

While the potatoes are cooking, cut the broccoli into small florets and cook in boiling salted water for about 10 minutes, or until soft. Drain and set aside.

In a wide frying pan, warm the olive oil and gently fry the chilli and garlic for 2–3 minutes over medium heat.

Add the potato and broccoli and season with salt and freshly ground black pepper. Push down on the vegetables with a large fork to create a rough, chunky purée. Cook for 5–6 minutes, or until the bottom is golden and the mixture is compact.

Carefully flip the torta over and cook for another 5–6 minutes, to lightly brown the other side.

Serve hot or cold.

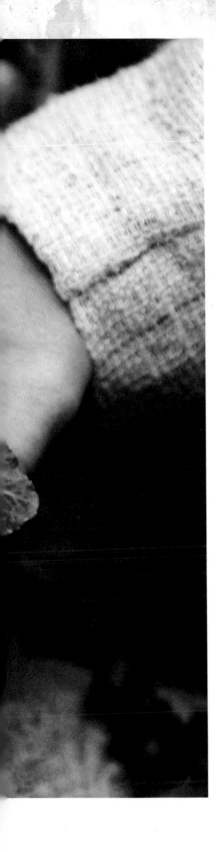

POMODORO COL RISO

(Rice-stuffed baked tomatoes)

BY TONI BRANCATISANO

**SERVES 4–6
AS AN APPETISER**

6 large ripe tomatoes

10 basil leaves, finely chopped

1 garlic clove, peeled

60 ml (2 fl oz/¼ cup) extra virgin olive oil, plus extra for drizzling

200 g (7 oz) Arborio rice

5–6 large floury/baking potatoes

When I think of my friend Toni, comfort food comes to mind. She is one of the best home cooks I know. She is always pottering away in the kitchen and her photos make me want to eat even the things I normally wouldn't — like *pomodoro col riso* (tomatoes with rice) or *pomodori ripieni* (stuffed tomatoes). I'm not a big tomato person (well, raw tomato actually), but I couldn't resist when Toni prepared these for me: tomatoes baked until soft and golden, serving as a little pot that cooks rice to perfection.

These tomatoes are great also because you can prepare them ahead of time.

Cut off the tops of the tomatoes, ensuring there will be sufficient space left to fill with rice. Reserve the lids. Use a spoon to remove the pulp from each tomato, placing the pulp in a bowl, and saving all the juice. Set the tomato shells aside.

Blend the pulp in a food processor and season with salt and freshly ground black pepper. Stir in the basil and garlic clove, along with half the olive oil.

Rinse the uncooked rice under running water, then stir into the tomato pulp and set aside to absorb for 1–1½ hours.

Preheat the oven to 180°C (350°F).

Peel the potatoes and cut them into equal-sized wedges. Place in a bowl, add the remaining olive oil and stir to coat well.

Put the tomato shells on a baking tray and drizzle with a little extra olive oil. Remove the whole garlic clove from the rice mixture, then spoon the rice into the tomato shells, filling to the brim. Brush the lids with olive oil and place them back on top of the tomatoes.

Add the potatoes to the tray, around the tomatoes, and bake for 1 hour, or up to 1 hour 20 minutes, until the rice is *al dente*.

Serve hot or lukewarm; they are also delicious eaten cold on a hot summer's day.

When I first tasted Angelo's fried anchovies with *pecorino* cheese, I thought I'd died and gone to heaven. They were salty, but not too salty, fried to perfection and addictive. I could not stop eating them. Angelo says his late dad, Emilio, used to make pasta with fresh anchovies and *pecorino*; again, a very unusual combination in the anti fish-and-cheese land of Italy. When Angelo started working in restaurants, he began playing with the same flavours by deep-frying the anchovies and sprinkling with *pecorino*. I personally think they are extra good because when I eat them, I can feel the love between a father and a son!

Eat them as soon as they come out of the frying pan.

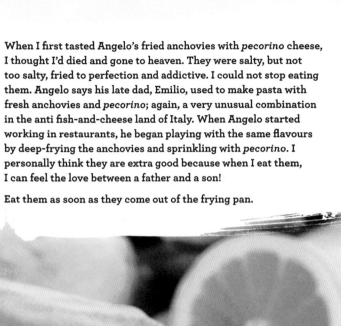

ALICI FRITTE CON PECORINO

(Fried anchovies with pecorino)

BY ANGELO PREZIOSI

SERVES 4

800 g (1 lb 12 oz) fresh anchovies (about 10–15 per person)

200 g (7 oz/1⅓ cups) plain (all-purpose) flour

vegetable oil, for deep-frying

100 g (3½ oz) Pecorino Romano, finely grated

1 small bunch Italian (flat-leaf) parsley, finely chopped

Prepare the anchovies by chopping off the heads, cutting down the belly and removing the interiors. Rinse under cold running water and place on a clean tea towel (dish towel) to drain, dabbing away any moisture with paper towel.

Place the flour on a large plate and individually coat each anchovy with a light dusting of flour.

Meanwhile, heat plenty of vegetable oil in a large heavy-based saucepan until boiling — about 170°C (340°F) on a cooking thermometer.

Working in several batches, fry the anchovies for 3–4 minutes, or until they just turn golden, stirring them with a slotted spoon so they colour evenly.

Drain on paper towel, place in a large bowl, sprinkle with the pecorino and parsley, and serve immediately.

CARPACCIO DI SPIGOLA

(Sea bass carpaccio)

BY OSTERIA DER BELLI

SERVES 4

600 g (1 lb 5 oz) sea bass fillets, or 1 kg (2 lb 3 oz) whole sea bass

100 ml (3½ fl oz) good-quality extra virgin olive oil, plus extra for drizzling

juice of 2 lemons

1 small handful rocket (arugula)

If using whole sea bass, remove the scales, then cut out the two fillets with a sharp knife, using the backbone as a guide. Carefully remove the skin, keeping the fillets intact, rinse and then remove any bones with kitchen tweezers.

Cut the fillets horizontally into thin slices, keeping the knife parallel with the work surface.

To make the dressing, whisk the olive oil and lemon juice in a small bowl until emulsified. Season with salt and freshly ground black pepper to taste.

Spoon some of the dressing over a plate or shallow dish, then lay out the slices of fish. Drizzle the remaining dressing over the top and sprinkle with the rocket.

Cover and leave to chill in the fridge for at least 3 hours.

Drizzle with a little more oil, sprinkle with salt and pepper and serve.

Only after moving to Italy did I learn about its long tradition of *crudi* (raw seafood). Historically, fishermen along Italy's extensive coastline would return to shore and eat their catch fresh. Italian *crudi* are different to the sashimi and raw fish of Japanese cuisine in that they are usually served with lemon or some sort of citrus juice, and extra virgin olive oil, salt and pepper.

This *carpaccio* of sea bass is my constant starter at Osteria der Belli in Trastevere. The lemon, oil and salt balance perfectly, and the fish just melts in the mouth. When making a *carpaccio* it's critical that you source the freshest and best-quality variety. The easiest way to prepare this dish is to buy your sea bass at the fishmonger already filleted and thinly sliced. You can prepare this dish ahead of your lunch or dinner, but know that it's not a dish that keeps.

CRISTINA BOWERMAN

Owner and Michelin-star chef at Glass Hostaria and Romeo E Giulietta

> "Traditions need to be protected, but also need to be treated as something you can nurture and play with. If they don't evolve with us, they die."

CRISTINA BOWERMAN, CHEF AND OWNER,
GLASS HOSTARIA AND ROMEO & GIULIETTA

I heard about Rome's only female Michelin-star chef, Cristina Bowerman, in 2011. I had just moved to Rome and lived on Vicolo del Cinque in Trastevere, right by her restaurant, Glass. In an area full of bars and *trattorie*, this place stood out. With its moody, modern interiors, it reminded me of Melbourne or New York.

Shortly after, I attended a cultural event that finished with a private lunch at Glass. The rest, as they say, is history. It has been my fine-dining go-to in Rome ever since, and I have brought many friends and family to enjoy the Bowerman experience — one that is cosmopolitan, distinctive, inspiring and above all, mouthwatering. Cristina was clearly born to live this life, but it took her a while to find that food was her passion.

Born in Cerignola, Puglia, in Italy's south, she always dreamt of bigger experiences and travel. Her parents sent her to an international school and she went on to become a lawyer. But an American holiday at the age of 26 would change the course of her life forever.

'After three days in the US, I called my parents from New York and said, "I'm not coming back".' Needing an excuse to stay, she enrolled to do her Master of Laws at the University of San Francisco. Enthralled with American culture, she immersed herself into local life; this would become the very foundation for the international and outward-looking approach she continues to apply to her craft today.

With a growing interest in food, Cristina started doing odd jobs in restaurants. She landed a lucrative stint at an American high-end restaurant consortium where, for the first time, she was exposed to new dining experiences and the world of restaurant management (from design, to marketing, to front of house). This stirred something creative in her and saw her take a job in graphic design in Austin, Texas. It was here that cooking started to turn from hobby to career.

'Austin is full of foodies. I'm Italian, so my friends would always ask me to cook. I saw it as a joke... just a little bit of fun. But then I realised it was probably more than that.' To further her skills, she gained a degree in Culinary Arts at the University of Austin (a program of the famed Parisian school, Le Cordon Bleu). She eventually returned to Italy with the intention of gaining Italian experience to take back to the US and open a restaurant there. However, it would seem destiny had other plans for her.

Speaking to her in her adopted Rome, it's hard to believe that someone who is all but a celebrity now on the Italian dining scene is so humble and gracious. When she was awarded her first Michelin star for Glass in 2009, she was the only woman that year. 'It's amazing how a star can change your life. Everything from the perception of you, the scrutiny and the pressure.'

Walking with her around the fresh food market in Rome's working class Testaccio neighbourhood, it's evident that stall owners love and respect her. Of the market she says, 'Not only do I get a lot of my stuff here, it's where I get a lot of my ideas.'

With her restaurant ventures in Rome (including the 2017 opening of Romeo e Giulietta, the biggest restaurant the city has ever seen), she continues to be cutting edge and push culinary boundaries in a country steeped in tradition. But she says despite the strong sense of tradition in Rome, there is still a place for innovation. 'Traditions need to be protected, but also need to be treated as something you can nurture and play with. If they don't evolve with us, they die.'

She encourages the people on her team to travel, get out of their comfort zone and contemplate living abroad. 'Only by experiencing different cultures and ways of life can you truly understand your place in the world and find out what your calling is.'

Spaghetti alle vongole means Italian summer to me. Nothing makes me happier than a plate of it at the beach. When I asked Leo, the owner of my favourite fish *osteria* in Trastevere, for his *spaghetti alle vongole* recipe, he was taken aback. He thought I'd have asked him for something more elaborate; something with an 'actual recipe'. That is the humility and simplicity of cuisine in Italy, because *spaghetti alle vongole* isn't all equal and, in my opinion, Leo's is extra special.

Dishes like these that seem simple to someone who has made it or eaten it all their life actually require a bit of practice for those of us who haven't. I love the version at Osteria der Belli because it has just the right hint of chilli and lots of clams.

Remember to clean your clams well, and always have some bread handy to mop up the delightful sauce afterwards.

SPAGHETTI ALLE VONGOLE

(Spaghetti with clams)

BY OSTERIA DER BELLI

SERVES 4

---

1 kg (2 lb 3 oz) clams (vongole)

---

500 g (1 lb 2 oz) spaghetti

---

60 ml (2 fl oz/¼ cup) extra virgin olive oil

---

125 ml (4 fl oz/½ cup) dry white wine

---

2 garlic cloves, finely chopped

---

2 red chillies, seeded and chopped

---

1 small bunch Italian (flat-leaf) parsley, chopped

Rinse the clams under cold water, discarding any that are broken or open.

Bring a large saucepan of salted water to the boil. Add the pasta and cook for the time indicated on the packet.

While the pasta is cooking, heat half the olive oil in a large, lidded frying pan. Add the clams to the pan, along with the wine. Cover and cook over high heat for about 1 minute, until the clams open and release their juices.

Remove the clams from the pan with a slotted spoon, discarding any that have not opened, and set aside. Pour the leftover juices through a fine sieve and set aside.

Heat the remaining olive oil in the same pan and add the garlic and chilli. Cook over low heat for 2–3 minutes, to gently infuse the oil without burning the garlic.

Add the strained clam juice and half the parsley, then turn up the heat and allow to reduce for 1 minute, until the sauce becomes almost creamy.

Add the cooked clams and cook for 30 seconds. Add the drained spaghetti, mixing well to coat the pasta in the sauce and evenly distribute the clams.

Serve with the remaining parsley sprinkled on top.

PESCE IN GUAZZETTO

(Fish stew)

BY FEDERICO DELMONTE, RISTORANTE CHINAPPI

SERVES 4

Fish

6 x 150 g (5½ oz) scorpion fish, or 800 g (1 lb 12 oz) fish fillets

3 oregano sprigs

50 ml (1¾ fl oz) dry white wine

75 ml (2½ fl oz) extra virgin olive oil

500 g (1 lb 2 oz) tomatoes

1 garlic glove, crushed

Crostini

12 slices rustic bread

1 garlic clove, peeled

extra virgin olive oil, for drizzling

1 small bunch Italian (flat-leaf) parsley, roughly chopped

Federico Delmonte is a young and talented chef from Italy's Le Marche region, and the dishes he creates for Rome's seafood dining institution, Chinappi, are quite delicate in flavour. This recipe — fish fillets cooked in a tomato and white wine sauce — is the same in that he doesn't play around too much with herbs, but throws in just the right amount to keep it simple.

Guazzetto is tricky to describe; it contains a lot of liquid (hence the chef's suggestion to serve with freshly toasted bread), but it's not really a soup. If you can't find scorpion fish, any meaty fish such as monkfish, snapper, bream, swordfish or mullet are good alternatives.

Fillet the scorpion fish — or ask your fishmonger to do this — and put the fillets in a bowl with the oregano. Pour over the wine and 2 tablespoons of the olive oil. Season with salt and freshly ground black pepper, mix gently and set aside.

Peel the tomatoes by scoring a cross on the bottom of each one, put them in a heatproof bowl and cover with boiling water. Leave for 30 seconds, then move them to a bowl of cold water and remove the skins by peeling away from the cross. Cut the tomatoes in half and use a spoon to scoop out the seeds. Chop the tomatoes and set aside.

Gently heat the remaining oil in a frying pan with the garlic for 1 minute. Add the chopped tomatoes and a little salt and pepper, and cook over medium heat for 4–5 minutes. Add the fish fillets, along with their marinade. Cover and continue to cook over medium–low heat for 10 minutes.

Meanwhile, make the crostini. Toast the bread, rub with the garlic clove, drizzle with olive oil and sprinkle with salt and the parsley.

Serve the fish stew in bowls, with the crostini to soak up the sauce.

Chapter
Five

LA
PIZZ

Naples might be Italy's capital of pizza, but quite frankly, Romans don't care. They are extremely proud and protective of their beloved *pizza Romana*. It is different to the Neapolitan style in that the flour differs, as does the yeast and fermentation process, and even the oil that is used. Pizza in Napoli has a thicker crust or lip, while *pizza Romana* is paper-thin and just about charred on the edges. In fact, I've sat at many a *pizzeria* in Rome with friends from out of town who have commented that their 'pizza is burnt'. In Rome, the more burnt, the better!

Romans distinguish their *pizza* from all others, calling it *pizza Romana*, or in Roman dialect, *la scrocchiarella*, which refers literally to its crunchiness.

Like everywhere else in Italy, in Rome, *pizza* is served as an individual portion on a plate. Rarely is the *pizza* cut; that's your job! When one refers to *pizza Romana* it's of the round kind (*pizza tonda*).

You will never find more than two or three toppings on a pizza, and the menu is usually divided by *pizze rosse* (red) or *pizze biancha* (white) to indicate pizza with tomato sauce or without. Romans generally eat pizza at dinner, and for this reason, many of the city's historic or neighbourhood *pizzerie* open only in the evening.

Other types of *pizza* found in Rome include *pizza al taglio* (by the slice) and the *pinsere* (an oblong-shaped pizza).

Pizza by the slice is sold by weight, and it's now common to find many outlets in Rome flirting with less traditional ingredients. At a *pizza al taglio* joint, you choose your pizza and the server cuts your desired portion, weighs it and warms it up. Then, depending on whether you want to take it away (*d'asportare* or *da portare via*) or to eat on the street (*in piedi*, literally 'on your feet'), it is wrapped and off you go! It's quick and easy, and the Italian version of take-out.

The *pinsere* is an ancient Roman style of pizza that's been around longer than pizza itself. The word *pinsere* derives from the Latin word for stretching, hence its long oblong shape. Also wood-fired and with most of the toppings you'd find in any *pizzeria*, it's less common on the streets of Rome, but worth a try if you're in town.

Going out for pizza in Rome is one of the most common dining options for large groups. With the European and broader global economic crisis that has crippled Italy on many levels, unemployment — especially among young Romans — is high, and working wages are extremely low compared to many foreign or European Union countries. This has had an indelible impact on the social lives of many Romans, who remain particularly budget conscious. The *pizzeria* therefore remains an extremely popular option for a quality meal that won't set you back more than €20 — and at many reputable outlets, even less.

As with most rituals around food, there's a process when you order and eat at a *pizzeria* in Rome. The first thing to know is that the meal here always starts off with *fritti* (fried food), and you won't find a *pizzeria* in Rome without a selection on the menu. The most common items include *fiori di zucca* (zucchini/courgette flowers stuffed with mozzarella and anchovy), *filetti di baccalà* (salt cod fillets), *mozzarelline* (crumbed mozzarella balls), *olive ascolane* (crumbed olive balls) and *supplì* (rice balls). Romans usually wash down fried food and *pizza* with beer, as opposed to wine.

There is a saying about the bill too. Paying *alla Romana* (Roman-style) means splitting the bill equally, irrespective of what you ate or drank. Romans hate a fuss when it comes to paying, therefore this is the preferred and easiest way.

Everyone in Rome debates where to find the best pizza and for the most part, people flock to their neighbourhood outlets. As in the *trattoria*, your local *pizzeria* staff treat you like family. My local *pizzerie* are Ai Marmi and Da Ivo in Trastevere, and I also love Da Remo in Testaccio. Reda, one of the waiters at Da Ivo, recently told me that he has been on the job for 24 years. 'The thing I love most about the *pizzeria*,' he explains, 'is that as waiters, we get to be ourselves, and relax and have fun with clients. A *pizzeria* isn't as formal as a restaurant.'

I regularly recommend Ai Marmi for visitors because it's a Trastevere (and Roman) institution. The real name of this bustling *pizzeria* is Pannatoni, but locals know it as L'Orbitorio (the morgue) or Ai Marmi (marble tabletops) in reference to its long marble tables. I love the old-school lit-up menu sign. There is always a queue (which moves fairly quickly), and I tell people to be prepared to sit elbow-to-elbow, which is all part of the fun!

When in Rome…

BASIC PIZZA DOUGH AND TOMATO SAUCE

BY ALICE KIANDRA ADAMS

MAKES 4 PIZZAS

Basic pizza dough

500 g (1 lb 2 oz/3⅓ cups) plain (all-purpose) flour

2 teaspoons dried yeast

1 teaspoon salt

½ teaspoon sugar

400 ml (13½ fl oz) tepid water

extra virgin olive oil, for greasing

Basic tomato sauce

500 g (1 lb 2 oz) tomato passata (puréed tomatoes)

2 tablespoons extra virgin olive oil

pinch of dried oregano or shredded basil

To make the dough, sift the flour into a large bowl, or the bowl of an electric stand mixer. Add the yeast, salt and sugar. Pour in the water and, if you are using a mixer, start to mix using the dough hook. If working by hand, start mixing with a fork, then use your hands to start bringing the ingredients together. If the dough is too wet, add a little extra flour.

When the dough is well mixed, turn it out onto a clean, floured surface and knead gently to form a ball. Place in a lightly greased bowl and cover with greased plastic wrap to stop the dough sticking when it rises.

The dough should take about 2 hours to rise. If the weather is warm it will rise easily; if it is cold, leave it in a warm spot near the oven or over a heater.

Once risen, turn the dough out onto a clean, floured surface and knead gently. Divide the dough into four portions. Cover with a damp tea towel (dish towel) and leave to rest while you prepare the toppings.

Preheat the oven to 240°C (465°F).

Each piece of dough can be rolled or hand stretched, depending on your preferred base. Rolling will create a thinner crust, while pulling the dough into shape by hand will maintain the air pockets and create a thicker crust.

Mix the passata and olive oil together in a small bowl. Add the herbs and a pinch of salt. Spread over the pizza bases, leaving a 2 cm (¾ inch) border around the edge.

Add your chosen toppings and bake for 10–15 minutes, until the dough starts turning lightly golden.

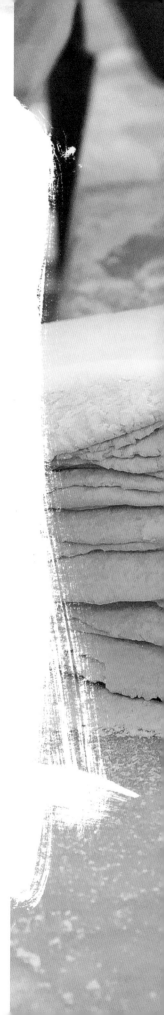

Alice Kiandra Adams is a good friend, fellow Melbourne girl, and has been living in Rome for over a decade. She is an extremely talented cook and food stylist and worked on this book with me. She was given this recipe by the father of one of her Roman friends, who was a baker in Trastevere for many years. She says he still directs the pizza-making at family get togethers in the countryside where they have a wood-fired oven, the key to wonderful pizza.

This is a very basic recipe, with easy-to-use dried yeast and a rising time of only 2 hours. It makes four round pizzas, which you can use to make any of the recipes in this chapter. I've included five of my favourites from the classics you will find on *pizzeria* menus in Rome.

MARGHERITA

MAKES 4 PIZZAS

1 quantity Basic pizza dough (page 152)

1 quantity Basic tomato sauce (page 152)

500 g (1 lb 2 oz) fresh mozzarella, chopped

basil leaves, to garnish

Preheat the oven to 240°C (465°F).

Top each pizza with the tomato sauce, then the mozzarella.

Bake for 10–15 minutes, until the dough starts turning lightly golden.

Garnish with basil leaves and serve.

MARINARA

MAKES 4 PIZZAS

1 quantity Basic pizza
dough (page 152)

1 quantity Basic tomato
sauce (page 152), made
with oregano

4 garlic cloves, thinly sliced

4 teaspoons dried oregano

extra virgin olive oil, for
drizzling

Preheat the oven to 240°C (465°F).

Top each pizza with the tomato sauce, then sprinkle with the
garlic and oregano.

Drizzle with olive oil and bake for 10–15 minutes, until the dough
starts turning lightly golden.

JEWISH-ROMAN CUISINE

and the Roman ghetto

Tucked away in the heart of Rome is the Jewish Ghetto, and while it is truly one of the most beautiful attractions of the city, it's perhaps one of the least well known. Lesser known still is that there is a whole Roman-Jewish cuisine that has intrinsically weaved its way into the mainstream Roman dining scene.

The Roman-Jewish community is regarded as one of the oldest in Europe, and the thriving Jewish Ghetto has shaped many aspects of the city and Roman life.

Established in 1555, the Ghetto combines Jewish culture with the beauty of Roman architecture and the ruins of the ancient *Portico d'Ottavia*. It sits within the *rione* (district) of Sant'Angelo, near the Tiber River, just across from Trastevere and south of Campo de' Fiori. It was originally cut off from the rest of the city by walls, which came down in 1888.

During Nazi occupation, the area was completely destroyed. History has it that the German government committed to sparing the deportation of Rome's Jews in exchange for a gold ransom (that the Vatican is said to have contributed to). The community raised the amount but on 16 October 1943, the Nazis deported approximately 2000 Jews from the Ghetto to Auschwitz. There are many stories of others who were taken in by Roman families or local churches, and a small number even took refuge within the Vatican City.

As part of a Europe-wide art project to honour victims of the holocaust, a gold cobblestone for each deportee sits in front of their last known residence. In Italian, they are called *pietre d'inciampo* (stumbling stones), and they are a touching, powerful and constant reminder of the past.

LAURA RAVAIOLI

Chef and TV presenter

Laura Ravaioli is a Roman chef, TV presenter and expert in all things Roman-Jewish. Born in Rome, she says she was practically raised in her *nonna's trattoria*, and credits her mother and grandmother as her first cooking teachers and inspiration.

One of her first jobs was as chef at Rome's then-famous Hemingway restaurant, and so began a career that took her into kitchens across the world, from Asia to New Zealand, the United States and Israel. Her current TV show, *Kasher* (shortened from the Roman dialectal term for kosher, *kashere*) showcases the recipes of the Roman-Jewish tradition, and the people and stories behind the Jewish Ghetto.

Laura says Rome's Jewish community remains strongly tied to the Ghetto. Here you find the synagogue, Jewish primary and secondary schools, kosher butchers, specialty food stores, bakeries and more. The traditions of the past have evolved, yet remain intrinsically linked to religious custom. Locals and tourists alike come to observe, celebrate, eat and pray here.

Restaurants and food outlets in the Ghetto abide by kosher rules and are monitored by local authorities to ensure they adhere to regulations in order to claim their authenticity. Walking the streets of the Ghetto in Rome, you will notice that restaurants and shops have their certificates proudly displayed on windowfronts and doors — take note if you're on the lookout for real Roman-Jewish fare.

In Rome, the recipes of the Jewish tradition appear on menus, not just in the Ghetto area,

but throughout the entire city. In particular, double-fried artichokes, *carciofi alla giudia* (Jewish-style), are a local favourite (page 20). Generally speaking, anything fried at a kosher restaurant in Rome is going to be good! Other dishes that can be found on menus at home or in the Ghetto include *aliciotti con l'indivia* (an anchovy and endive bake, page 128), *stracotto alla giudia* (a slow-cooked beef stew, page 42) and *la concia* (a fried zucchini specialty, page 130).

Laura maintains that Rome's Jewish Ghetto is one of the most authentic parts of the city to eat in because menus are a carbon copy of what is still cooked at home; dishes that focus on simplicity and fresh produce.

She is proud of her Jewish faith and heritage, one she reconnected with as an adult, given that prior to the Second World War, her entire family had converted to Catholicism in response to the anti-Semitic climate of the time.

Nostalgically she recounts tales of the Ghetto and the personalities that make it the vibrant melting pot it is today. One of her favourite stories is about Shabbat (sabbath), when families who couldn't afford to use gas at home would head down to the Boccione bakery (still an institution to this day) to use the ovens. Word on the street is that some people returned to find that someone in the neighbourhood had sneakily taken their dishes in exchange for their own; the more luxurious items like lamb would somehow just disappear.

She speaks fondly of a community that remains proud and defiant in spite of a tumultuous and heart-wrenching past — a community that is as much a part of Rome as any monument, cobblestone or ruin.

"Rome's Jewish community remains strongly tied to the Ghetto. Here you find the synagogue, Jewish primary and secondary schools, kosher butchers, specialty food stores, bakeries and more."

LAURA RAVAIOLI
CHEF AND TV PRESENTER

BOSCAIOLA

MAKES 4 PIZZAS

1 quantity Basic pizza
dough (page 152)

1 quantity Basic tomato
sauce (page 152)

500 g (1 lb 2 oz) fresh
mozzarella, chopped

200 g (7 oz) button
mushrooms, thinly sliced

2 pork sausages

Preheat the oven to 240°C (465°F).

Top each pizza with the tomato sauce, then the mozzarella. Arrange the sliced mushrooms around.

Remove the casings from the sausages. Roughly chop the meat, then divide among the pizzas.

Bake for 10–15 minutes, until the dough starts turning lightly golden.

FIORI DI ZUCCA E ALICI

MAKES 4 PIZZAS

10 zucchini (courgette) flowers

1 quantity Basic pizza dough (page 152)

500 g (1 lb 2 oz) fresh mozzarella, chopped

24 anchovy fillets in olive oil

Preheat the oven to 240°C (465°F).

Remove the stems and stamens from the zucchini flowers. Gently open the flowers out flat, then cut into 2–3 cm (¾–1¼ inch) strips.

Top each pizza with the mozzarella.

Arrange six anchovies on each pizza and top with the strips of zucchini flower.

Bake for 10–15 minutes, until the dough starts turning lightly golden.

FIORI DI ZUCCA E SALSICCIA

MAKES 4 PIZZAS

10 zucchini (courgette) flowers

1 quantity Basic pizza dough (page 138)

500 g (1 lb 2 oz) fresh mozzarella, chopped

2 pork sausages

Preheat the oven to 240°C (465°F).

Remove the stems and stamens from the zucchini flowers. Gently open the flowers out flat, then cut into 2–3 cm (¾–1¼ inch) strips.

Top each pizza with the mozzarella.

Remove the casings from the sausages. Roughly chop the meat, then divide among the pizzas.

Scatter with the zucchini flowers and bake for 10–15 minutes, until the dough starts turning lightly golden.

169

Chapter Six

IL QUI QUA

While *carbonara*, *amatriciana*, *cacio e pepe*, fried *baccalà* (salt cod), *fiori di zucca* (stuffed zucchini/ courgette flowers), fried artichokes and *saltimbocca alla Romana* are some of the more popular Roman dishes, they are actually considered to be modern. The true historic *cucina Romana* is predominantly offal, or what is often known as nose-to-tail — the parts left over after butchers have taken all the prime cuts.

This type of *cucina Romana* is often referred to as the *quinto quarto*, which literally translates as the 'fifth quarter'. It dates back to the late 1800s, when workers at the slaughterhouse in the working-class-cum-gentrified neighbourhood of Testaccio were literally paid in animal parts.

Animal carcasses are butchered into quarters, and meat goods were historically divided equally among four different classes — the nobility, the clergy, the bourgeois and the military. Whatever was left became colloquially known as the 'fifth quarter', and was what the workers would take home to their wives. Rome therefore saw a generation of women who had to creatively make-do with what they were given to feed their families, and so the real *cucina Romana* — *quinto quarto* — was born!

Dishes such as *trippa alla Romana* (tripe cooked in a rich tomato sauce) and *coratella* (pan-fried lamb heart, lungs, liver, spleen and parts of the oesophagus) can still be found on *trattoria* menus across Rome. My favourite of the set is *coda alla vaccinara* — slow-cooked or braised oxtail in

a rich tomato sauce made with carrot, celery and cocoa. Some recipes include raisins and pine nuts to provide even more texture.

La pajata is the pan-fried intestines of unweaned baby calves, served in a rich tomato sauce. It made headlines in the early 2000s when the European Union banned it after the spread of Mad Cow disease. But in 2015, offal-loving Romans rejoiced as the ban was lifted and the dish returned to *trattoria* menus.

While these dishes have never been out of fashion in Rome, they do seem to have become more in vogue of late, especially among young Romans. Many of the classics are being reincarnated with modern twists. For instance, at many street food carts or market stands you'll find tripe as a filling for gourmet sandwiches, or as the stuffing in one of Rome's favourite street food snacks, the *trapizzino* (a delicious pizza pocket). At Testaccio Market local hotspot, Mordi e Vai, their *panini* stuffed with either tripe or tongue sell by the dozen daily.

If I'm being honest, offal is not really my thing, but I'll try anything once. And as an adopted Roman I saw it as a rite of passage to sample the lot. Now, while I never wake up in the morning craving the stuff, if *coda alla vaccinara* is on the menu, especially as a sauce served with gnocchi, you can absolutely count me in!

TRIPPA ALLA ROMANA

(Roman-style tripe)

BY TONI BRANCATISANO

SERVES 6

900 g (2 lb) tripe, cleaned and blanched (see Note)

2 lemons, cut into quarters

50 ml (1¾ fl oz) extra virgin olive oil

1 red onion, thinly sliced

2 garlic cloves, coarsely chopped

125 ml (4 fl oz/½ cup) dry white wine

800 g (1 lb 12 oz) tinned chopped tomatoes

1 carrot, halved

20 mint leaves, finely chopped

100 g (3½ oz) Pecorino Romano, grated, plus extra to serve

Put the tripe in a large saucepan and cover with water. Bring to the boil and cook for 10 minutes, then drain into a colander and run under cold water until cool. Place in a bowl, cover with cold water, add the lemon quarters and leave for 30 minutes.

Heat the olive oil in a large saucepan. Add the onion and garlic and cook over low heat for about 5 minutes, or until the onion is translucent. Add the wine and allow to reduce a little before adding the tomatoes and carrot. Season with salt and freshly ground black pepper, then cover and cook for 30 minutes. Remove the carrot halves.

Remove the tripe from the water and slice into bite-sized strips, about 1 cm (½ inch) wide. Add the tripe to the tomatoes and leave to simmer for 1 hour.

Add half the mint, stirring well, then cover and simmer for a further 1 hour, or until very tender.

In a small bowl, mix together the remaining mint and pecorino.

Remove the tripe from the heat and stir through the pecorino and mint. Taste and adjust the seasoning if necessary.

Serve with an extra sprinkling of pecorino, with bread to mop up all the lovely juices.

✳ NOTE: In Rome, you can buy tripe cleaned and blanched. Any butcher will clean it, but if yours hasn't already been blanched, here's what you do. Cut your tripe into about six pieces to make it easier to handle, then rinse under cold water for a minute. Place in a large saucepan and pour in 3 litres (101 fl oz/12 cups) cold water and 150 ml (5 fl oz) white vinegar. Add 1 tablespoon fine salt and slowly bring to the boil. Leave to simmer for 15 minutes, then drain into a colander and leave to cool.

Of the Roman offal collection, tripe is the most mainstream. Compared to intestines and pan-fried spleen, cow stomach lining seems kind of tame! My friend Toni isn't Roman, but her partner is, so she has perfected this dish over the years and it's now at a standard that Alberto is satisfied with. I trust Alberto's authenticity stamp, given it's his birthright to know good tripe!

This is a signature dish in Rome and is often chalked up on *trattoria* blackboards about town. Cooked in a rich tomato sauce, I know you'll love Toni's classic version.

"Rome is the city of echoes, the city of illusions, and the city of yearning."

— GIOTTO DI BONDONE

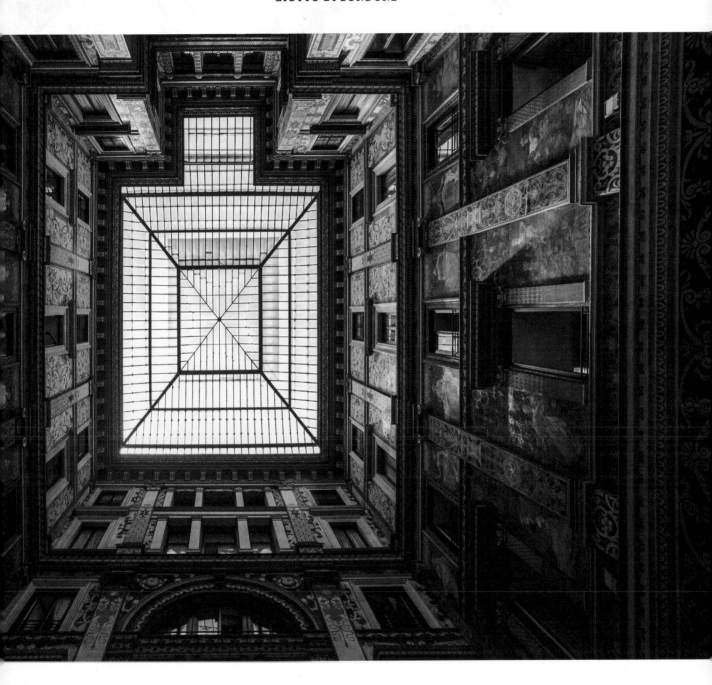

This is my favourite of the *cucina Romana* nose-to-tail set: slow-cooked or braised oxtail in a rich tomato sauce. The Romans refer to it as *la regina del quinto quarto* — the queen of the offal collection! The name refers to the *vaccinaro* (the cattle butcher), and dates back to the late 1800s, when it was customary to pay the butcher in animal parts. It's usually made with carrot, celery and cocoa, and some recipes, such as this one from Da Enzo al 29 in Trastevere, includes raisins and pine nuts, for an even more delicious texture. I've added carrot to their recipe because I prefer it.

A wonderful sharing dish, this is Roman comfort food at its finest — the meat literally pulls apart and melts in your mouth. Don't let the sauce go to waste; put it aside to serve with pasta, such as *gnocchi* or *rigatoni*.

CODA ALLA VACCINARA

(Roman-style oxtail stew)

BY DA ENZO AL 29

SERVES 6

3 kg (6 lb 10 oz) oxtail pieces

1 kg (2 lb 3 oz) celery stalks, trimmed

600 g (1 lb 5 oz) carrots, peeled

60 ml (2 fl oz/¼ cup) extra virgin olive oil

125 ml (4 fl oz/½ cup) dry white wine

2 kg (4 lb 6 oz) tinned chopped tomatoes

2 tablespoons pine nuts

2 tablespoons raisins

dark unsweetened cocoa powder, for sprinkling

Rinse the oxtail pieces well and blot up any excess moisture with paper towel. Roughly cut the celery and carrots into chunky strips about 8 cm (3¼ inches) long.

Heat the olive oil in a large heavy-based saucepan. Add the oxtail pieces and fry in batches over high heat for 4–5 minutes until browned, turning to colour each side, removing each batch to a plate.

Add the wine, celery and carrot to the pan, stirring to deglaze the pan, and cook for another minute. Stir in the tomatoes. Return all the oxtail pieces to the pan and season well with salt and freshly ground black pepper.

Reduce the heat to medium–low and leave to simmer for about 3½–4 hours, stirring occasionally. The stew is ready when the meat easily comes away from the bone and the sauce is thick.

Taste and adjust the seasoning if necessary. Stir in the pine nuts and raisins, and sprinkle with a little cocoa powder before serving.

CORATELLA

(Lamb offal with onions)

BY ANGELO PREZIOSI

SERVES 4

2 sets of lamb offal
(lungs, heart, spleen, liver)

100 ml (3½ fl oz)
extra virgin olive oil

2 onions, sliced

125 ml (4 fl oz/½ cup)
dry white wine

Coratella can usually be found on the menu only at the most authentic Roman *trattorie*, as it's a little too adventurous for those catering to a more touristy market. This pan-fried delicacy of lamb heart, lungs, liver and spleen is cooked in stages to get the texture right for all components. For Angelo it is a springtime staple, and his family have it on the menu as part of their breakfast blowout on Easter Sunday, along with *salumi*, cheese, and *pizza di Pasqua al formaggio*, a cheese bread eaten typically at Easter.

Rinse all the offal well. Keeping the different organs separate, chop them into 1–2 cm (½–¾ inch) pieces.

Heat the olive oil in a large frying pan. Add the onion and cook over medium heat for 7–8 minutes, until just starting to turn golden, being careful not to let the onion burn.

Add the lungs and cook for 5 minutes, before adding the heart. Cook for another 3 minutes, then add the spleen.

After another 3 minutes, add the liver and season everything well with salt and freshly ground black pepper.

Allow to gently cook together for 5 minutes, taking care to avoid burning or drying out; the offal and onions should be silky smooth and tender.

Add the wine and simmer for a few more minutes, until the alcohol has evaporated.

Serve immediately.

STEFANO CALLEGARI

Trapizzino founder and pizza-maker

In 2008, renowned Roman *pizzaiolo* Stefano Callegari invented the *trapizzino*, transforming the ingredients of home-cooked Roman cuisine to an inexpensive meal you can eat on the run. It has fast become a favourite street food snack for Romans, the name a play on words between *pizza* and the Italian word for a triangle-shaped sandwich, *tramezzino*. It's a pizza pocket of sorts (a triangle-shaped *pizza bianca*) that comes filled with things you might find in *Nonna's* kitchen, in particular, specialties such as Roman-style offal. There are currently about 30 varieties, including *trippa alla Romana* (tripe), tongue with *salsa verde*, vegetable *caponata*, burrata with zucchini (courgette), and broccoli with pork sausage.

Stefano was born in Rome in 1968 to a family not unfamiliar with the restaurant sector. He credits this for the many cooking secrets that stuck with him since childhood. In the early to mid-1990s he started doing delivery runs for a bakery where he shadowed the bakers, seeking to learn the tricks of the trade from them, and then finally enrolled in a professional pizza-making course.

In 2005, together with some friends (his now business partners: Antonio Pratticò, Paul Pansera and Fabio Giacomobono), he opened his first *pizzeria* in Rome, Sforno. Then came 00100 Pizza, Tonda and more recently, Sbanco.

At his sit-down *pizzeria* restaurants, it's not just the classics on the menu, but his famous 'Greenwich' with port reduction and Stilton blue cheese, decadent *carbonara* pizza and the unique *cacio e pepe*. Here, Stefano transforms the Roman classic pasta dish into a pizza, but it took him a while to get the right creamy consistency. He knew that the key to the perfect *cacio e pepe* is the starchy water the pasta has been boiled in, but says he couldn't put water on a pizza base. In the end, he tried ice cubes. It was a success. As the cubes melted in the wood-fired oven and mixed with the *pecorino* and pepper, he had the *cacio e pepe* effect he'd been looking for.

Slowly, Stefano's name and all of his brands have become synonymous with quality pizza in Rome. But it was at 00100 — a tiny pizza-by-the-slice joint in Rome's food heartland, the Testaccio neighbourhood — where the *trapizzino* came to life. Since opening in 2008, the *trapizzino* gained popularity so rapidly that in 2013, the outlet underwent a complete rebrand, and three dedicated Trapizzino outlets have since opened in Rome, with a fourth on its way.

Stefano says their success is linked to nostalgia and food memory. 'The *trapizzino* combines delicious *pizza bianca* with the dishes of the past, a winning combination. For years here in Italy we have become increasingly fascinated with international cuisine and trends, but somehow forgotten about the wholesomeness and goodness of our own.'

He says that in a sense, the *trapizzino* brings the Italian colloquial term *scarpetta* to life. Translating to 'little shoe', it's the word used to describe the mopping up of whatever sauce is left on your plate. Quite often, the *trapizzino* is filled with juicy, sauce-based dishes, and the servers make sure that the pizza pocket has been soaked before it's filled for extra flavour!

Trapizzino was recently featured at some events in Australia, and the first American store has just opened in New York City. It seems Stefano's dream of taking *cucina Romana* to the world is in full flight.

Let's say I have a funny story to tell about *la pajata*, the pan-fried intestines of baby calves that are often served with *rigatoni* and a rich tomato sauce. I tell it every time I'm asked if I like the dish. I answer truthfully: while I'm not an offal fan, I enjoyed *la pajata*, but I will never eat it again. I had a bad experience with it in that my significant other at the time brought it over to my place homemade — by his Roman mother — and then dumped me. Between the heartbreak and the courage it took to try baby calf intestines, let's say it left its mark.

This recipe is Angelo's, and he says that in the 14 years *la pajata* was banned by the European Union thanks to Mad Cow disease, butchers sold lamb intestine, but it wasn't the same. Despite the ban, his family continued to eat it at the time, thanks to a very special friendship with their butcher in Abruzzo, who would hide it under the counter for them (oohhhhh!).

Rest assured that if you see *la pajata* on a menu while dining in Rome, you are at a real-deal *trattoria*.

RIGATONI CON LA PAJATA

(Rigatoni with veal intestine)

BY ANGELO PREZIOSI

SERVES 4

800 g (1 lb 12 oz) baby calf intestine

½ celery stalk

1 small carrot

1 small onion

60 ml (2 fl oz/¼ cup) extra virgin olive oil

60 ml (2 fl oz/¼ cup) dry white wine

500 g (1 lb 2 oz) tomato passata (puréed tomatoes)

360 g (12½ oz) rigatoni

100 g (3½ oz) Pecorino Romano, grated, plus extra to serve

First, prepare the intestine by rinsing it well, then cutting it into lengths of about 10–15 cm (4–6 inches). Then, using kitchen string, tie the ends together to form little ring shapes, to keep the milk inside.

Finely dice the celery, carrot and onion. Heat the olive oil in a large heavy-based saucepan and gently fry the vegetables for 5 minutes, until beginning to soften. Add the rings of intestine and season with salt and freshly ground black pepper.

When the rings begin to brown slightly, add the wine, turn the heat up high and cook for 4–5 minutes.

Add the passata, reduce the heat to low and cook gently for 1½–2 hours, stirring occasionally, and making sure the sauce doesn't burn.

Just before serving, bring a large saucepan of salted water to the boil, add the pasta and cook for the time indicated on the packet.

Drain the pasta and gently mix through the sauce. Squeeze the now-curdled milk out of three or four of the intestine rings to thicken up the sauce and add extra flavour.

Sprinkle in the pecorino, then stir together well before serving with an extra dusting of cheese.

LINGUA CON SALSA VERDE

(Tongue with salsa verde)

BY ANGELO PREZIOSI

SERVES 4–6

1 veal tongue, weighing about 800 g (1 lb 12 oz)

1 celery stalk, cut into large chunks

1 onion, halved

1 carrot, halved

2 tablespoons salt

2 tablespoons whole black peppercorns

Salsa verde

1 bunch Italian (flat-leaf) parsley, roughly chopped

1 hard-boiled egg yolk

1 garlic clove

30 g (1 oz) white bread

60 ml (2 fl oz/¼ cup) white wine vinegar

100 ml (3½ fl oz) extra virgin olive oil

I had never tasted tongue until I moved to Rome. A waiter at a reputable restaurant in Rome's offal heartland of Testaccio convinced our group to do a tasting. Served with a mouthwatering salsa verde, my mental preconceptions were appeased and I remember thinking to myself, well at least I can say I've eaten tongue! Angelo says he usually prepares it the traditional way, but you could also mix thin slices of tongue with crunchy pickled vegetables to make a salad of sorts. His favourite way to eat it is stuffed into the soft *pizza bianca* pocket of a *trapizzino*.

Put the whole tongue into a large saucepan, along with the celery, onion, carrot, salt and peppercorns. Cover with cold water and bring to the boil. Leave to simmer for 1–1½ hours, or until cooked through. Test by sticking a fork into the side of the thick end of the tongue; it is ready when the tongue slides off the fork easily.

Once the tongue is cooked, but while it is still warm, remove the skin. Leave to cool, then cut into slices about 1 cm (½ inch) thick, ready to serve.

Meanwhile, prepare the salsa verde. Put the parsley, egg yolk and garlic in a bowl. Season with a little salt and freshly ground black pepper. Soak the bread quickly in the vinegar and squeeze to remove the excess liquid, before also adding to the bowl. Mix everything together with a hand-held stick blender, gradually drizzling in the olive oil. If the sauce is too watery, add a little more bread.

Drizzle the tongue with the salsa verde and serve.

LA
PASTIC

La pasticceria, the local cake shop, has always played an important role in Italian social and culinary culture. On a Sunday morning, one must stop off at *la pasticceria* to pick up some cakes to bring to your mamma (and especially your *suocera*, mother-in-law!) for lunch. There is rarely a meal had without something sweet to finish, and quite often, if I'm invited to friends for lunch or dinner, I will bring some small cakes, *pasticcini* or *mignon* (used commonly as a term in Italy, but taken from the French vocabulary).

At *la pasticceria*, you buy your cakes, or anything from chocolate to biscuits, nougat and even savoury pies, by weight. Yes, you select what you want and the shopkeeper weighs it and gives you a price based on their established price per gram. My favourite part comes next — the beautiful packaging that goes on in cake shops across Italy. While a cake might come in a pretty box, small cakes or biscuits are usually placed on a disposable tray, a cardboard arch is placed over the tray (to avoid a paper-meets-cake situation), and then the tray is wrapped with paper, ribbon and all.

As an incurable sweet tooth, you could say I'm a regular at my local *pasticceria*. The owner at Pasticceria Trastevere, Signora Vera, is one of my favourite women in Rome. She has a no-nonsense attitude and an extremely dry sense of humour. It took a while, but she's warmed to me.

One of the very first times I went into her shop, I bought a selection of small sweets to eat on the run. I couldn't decide between ones with custard (*crema*) or cream (*panna*). After selecting some custard ones, I then immediately changed my mind and asked if I could swap one for cream. Then I asked to swap a second one. Well at that point, in a pretty direct way — and so that the entire cake shop full of clients

could hear — she said to me in her thick Roman dialect, *Ao, se semmo capiti. A te piac a panna!* ('I got it girl, you like cream!')

It was the first of many funny moments, and at least once or twice (okay, maybe even three times) a week I pop in for a *mignon* (or two) — with whipped cream of course!

Around *le feste* (holiday periods), cake shops and bakeries across Rome are loaded with special sweets, because every celebration in Italy has its own sweet tradition.

At Easter and Christmas, you'll find ornately wrapped Easter eggs and *panettone* (a traditional Italian cake with dried fruit) as part of the store displays or hanging as decorations.

In the lead-up to Easter and *Carnevale* in Italy, *pasticcerie* are full of *frappe* or *castagnole*, with regional variations found across the country. *Frappe* are thin strips of pastry, baked or fried and dusted with icing (confectioners') sugar, also known elsewhere in Italy as *crostoli* or *chiacchiere*. *Castagnole* are literally balls of dough, like little round doughnuts, rolled in sugar and sometimes filled with custard or *ricotta*. The idea is that you eat as indulgently as you like until 40 days before Easter, when Lent — the period of abstinence — begins.

When it comes to sweets, you won't find anything overwhelmingly different in Rome than you would across other parts of Italy. Items such as *tiramisù* and *pannacotta* now transcend regional borders and are available throughout the country. However, one thing you will always find in *pasticcerie* all over Rome is the *maritozzo*. This Roman classic is not just a cream-filled bun, but the pride of the city.

While all the Italian classic desserts can be found in Rome, the *maritozzo* is probably one of the most loved and cherished Roman sweets, because many locals will tell you they taste of nostalgia! This former breakfast item of choice was superseded by the *cornetto* — Italy's version of a croissant, often jam or custard filled — but is now back in style. It's very common to see Romans hanging around late-night bakeries in the early hours, eating a *maritozzo* after a big night out. The name has a cute connotation in that it translates to 'almost married', and legend has it that young men would gift them to their bride-to-be.

This recipe is from Rome's premier bakery, Antico Forno Roscioli, which has been baking bread for the city since 1972 on a site that is said to have been a bakery as early as 1824. The leavening process for their *maritozzo* takes 24 hours, but the result is well worth it.

MARITOZZO CON PANNA

(Sweet cream buns)

BY ANTICO FORNO ROSCIOLI

MAKES 15–20

500 ml (17 fl oz/2 cups) whipping cream

icing (confectioners') sugar, for dusting

Buns

65 g (2¼ oz) caster (superfine) sugar

zest of ½ lemon, finely grated

½ vanilla bean

1 egg, plus 1 yolk

2 teaspoons fresh yeast

500 g (1 lb 2 oz/3⅓ cups) strong plain (all-purpose) white bread flour

250 ml (8½ fl oz/1 cup) water

65 g (2¼ oz) margarine

1 teaspoon salt

Sugar glaze

1 egg white

1 teaspoon lemon juice

200 g (7 oz) caster (superfine) sugar

100 ml (3½ fl oz) water

To make the buns, put the sugar and lemon zest in a bowl. Split the vanilla bean in half lengthways and carefully scrape the seeds into the bowl, using a teaspoon. Mix together and set aside. In a separate bowl, lightly beat the egg and extra yolk, then add in the fresh yeast.

Sift the flour into a large bowl, or the bowl of an electric stand mixer fitted with a dough hook. Gradually combine the water into the flour, pouring it in a steady stream until well mixed. Add the sugar mixture, and the yeast mixture, then also add the margarine and salt. Mix well on a low speed, or using your hands, until the dough is smooth and elastic. Transfer to a clean bowl, cover with plastic wrap and leave to rise in the fridge for 24 hours.

Once the dough has risen, turn it out onto a clean, well-floured surface and form into 15–20 oval balls of about 60 g (2 oz) each. Place them on a tray lined with baking paper and leave in a warm place for about 1 hour.

Preheat the oven to 200°C (400°F). Once the buns have doubled in size, bake them for 15 minutes, or until golden. Remove from the oven and transfer to a wire rack to cool while you make the glaze and whip the cream.

For the sugar glaze, beat the egg white lightly with the lemon juice and sugar. Transfer to a small saucepan, add the water and cook over medium heat for 5 minutes, continuing to mix well.

When the buns have cooled slightly, brush them with the sugar glaze.

When the buns have cooled completely, whip the cream in a bowl. Cut the buns lengthways down the middle, but not all the way through, leaving them hinged together. Fill with the cream and dust with icing sugar.

The unfilled buns will keep in an airtight container for several days, but should be filled only as you eat them, or they'll go soggy.

History has it that in the 16th century, while Jewish communities in northern Italy would sprinkle baked cheese sandwiches with sugar and cinnamon, Roman Jews used ricotta to make large sweet pancake-style sweets, which they called *casciola*, from the Roman dialect word for cheese, *cascio* (now *cacio*). As the dish evolved, so did the name, and it became *la cassola* — a baked cheesecake of sorts.

I was given this recipe by Carla Tomasi, who is an extraordinarily talented baker and cookery teacher. She says that like all baked cheesecakes, *la cassola* would benefit from a day of resting — especially if using cow's milk ricotta instead of the traditional sheep's milk ricotta, as it is wetter. So, if time allows, bake it the day before and let it sit overnight.

CASSOLA

(Baked cheesecake)

BY CARLA TOMASI

SERVES 6–8

650 g (1 lb 7 oz) cow's or
sheep's milk ricotta

butter, for greasing

flour, for dusting

5 eggs

300 g (10½ oz) sugar

zest of 1 lemon

icing (confectioners')
sugar, for dusting

The day before, or a few hours before you are planning to bake, put the ricotta in a fine-meshed sieve, or a colander lined with baking paper, and leave to drain.

Grease a deep, 20–22 cm (8–8¾ inch) springform cake tin and line with buttered baking paper. Lightly dust the inside of the tin with flour and tip out the excess. This will give the cake a fine crust.

Once the ricotta is well drained, push it through a sieve, or blend in a food processor until smooth. Spoon into a large mixing bowl.

Preheat the oven to 200°C (400°F).

Using an electric stand mixer or food processor, whisk together the eggs, sugar and lemon zest, until the mixture triples in volume.

Pour one-third of the egg mixture over the ricotta and lightly mix with a wire whisk to loosen the texture. Once the ricotta looks creamy, gently fold in the remaining egg mixture with a spoon, being careful not to knock the air out. The texture should be liquid and airy.

Pour the mixture into the prepared cake tin and bake for 10 minutes, then reduce the oven temperature to 160°C (320°F) and bake for another 30–35 minutes. The cake is ready when it is just firm to the touch, but still has a slight wobble.

Turn the oven off, open the door and leave the cake to settle for 20 minutes.

Wait at least a few hours before lightly dusting with icing sugar and serving, or keep in the fridge overnight and serve the next day.

"I found Rome a city of bricks and left it a city of marble."

— CAESAR AUGUSTUS, FOUNDER OF THE ROMAN EMPIRE

Said to date back to Roman times, *le frappe* can be found in cake shops, bakeries, supermarkets and homes across Rome during *Carnevale*. During this period, you're allowed to literally carb load in any way before the pre-Easter Lent period begins. In Australia I knew these as *crostoli*, and while their name might change throughout Italy — *crostoli, chiacchiere, bugie, sfrappole, frappe* — they are all the same deliciously fried, sweet pastry strips sprinkled with lots of icing sugar.

This is my friend Toni's recipe, and you'll have trouble stopping at one because they are so sweet and crispy.

LE FRAPPE

(Sweet pastry strips)

BY TONI BRANCATISANO

MAKES ABOUT 80

300 g (10½ oz/2 cups) plain (all-purpose) flour, plus extra for dusting

200 g (7 oz/1⅓ cups) self-raising flour

80 g (2¾ oz) sugar

3 whole eggs, plus 1 egg yolk, lightly beaten

2 tablespoons grappa

finely grated zest of 1 lemon

50 g (1¾ oz) butter, at room temperature

vegetable oil, for frying

icing (confectioners') sugar, for dusting

Sift the flours into the bowl of an electric stand mixer. Add the sugar, beaten eggs and egg yolk, grappa, lemon zest and a pinch of salt. Combine together well, then add the butter and mix using the dough hook until a dough forms.

Turn the dough out onto a clean lightly floured surface and knead with your hands for about 10 minutes, or until smooth. If the mixture is too dry, add a little water. Roll into a ball, cover with plastic wrap and leave to rest at room temperature for 30 minutes.

Divide the dough into four portions. Cover three of them with plastic wrap so they don't dry out. Set up a pasta machine on your table or worktop. Knead the fourth portion of dough and flatten it out a little with a rolling pin, then pass the dough through the pasta machine on its widest setting. Fold the dough into three, then pass it through the machine again. Continue to pass the dough through the pasta machine, turning the knob up a notch each time until you reach the thinnest setting. If you do not have a pasta machine you can roll out the dough by hand, making sure it is very thin.

Using a zig-zag pastry cutter, cut the pastry into strips measuring about 3 x 10 cm (1¼ x 4 inches). For each strip, cut a slit lengthways along the centre. Loop one end of the strip through the slit (or just leave as flat strips if you prefer). Leave them on a floured surface while you repeat the process with the remaining pieces of dough.

Once you've prepared all your *frappe*, leave them to rest while you heat plenty of vegetable oil in a large heavy-based saucepan until boiling — about 180°C (350°F) on a cooking thermometer.

Working quickly, add three *frappe* to the hot oil and fry for about 1–2 minutes, or until golden, turning them over with a slotted spoon to ensure an even colour. Remove and drain on paper towel. Fry the remaining frappe in the same way, then drain and leave to cool.

Serve sprinkled with icing sugar. The *frappe* will keep for up to 2 weeks in an airtight container, stored at room temperature.

I love *Carnevale* in Rome. In fact, all throughout Italy, sweet treats abound during this decadent, almost sinful, time of year. Basically, you won't be judged for eating as many *castagnole* as you like, because the idea is that as soon as Lent arrives, it's time to avoid all sugary temptation.

This recipe was given to me by Alice Kiandra Adams, a fellow Melbourne girl living in Rome. Alice is an extremely talented cook and food stylist and says be sure to coat your *castagnole* in sugar as soon as they come out of the pan, and eat them nice and hot.

CASTAGNOLE

(Fried doughnuts)

BY ALICE KIANDRA ADAMS

MAKES 35–40

---

60 g (2 oz) butter, softened

---

80 g (2¾ oz/⅓ cup) caster (superfine) sugar, plus extra for dusting (optional)

---

3 eggs

---

finely grated zest of 1 lemon

---

2 teaspoons baking powder

---

375 g (13 oz/2½ cups) plain (all-purpose) flour

---

vegetable oil, for frying

---

icing (confectioners') sugar, for dusting (optional)

In a large bowl, beat the softened butter with the caster sugar using a spoon. Add the eggs one at a time, mixing well before incorporating the next egg.

Add the lemon zest, baking powder and a pinch of salt, before gradually mixing in the flour until you have a smooth, soft dough. Wrap in plastic wrap and rest the dough for 30 minutes.

Use a teaspoon to scoop the dough into small chunks that can then be rolled into balls. They don't need to be particularly even, but don't make the balls too large or the insides may not cook through.

Half-fill a small, deep, heavy-based saucepan with vegetable oil and heat until boiling — about 180°C (350°F) on a cooking thermometer. If you plan to roll your hot *castagnole* in caster sugar, spread some sugar out on a plate.

Add the dough balls to the hot oil in batches and cook for about 3–5 minutes, or until golden, stirring them with a slotted spoon so they colour evenly. Scoop them out with the slotted spoon.

If rolling them in caster sugar, drop them in straight away, so that the sugar sticks to the just-fried surface. Alternatively, you can let them cool a little and sprinkle with icing sugar.

CAFFÈ E DIGESTIVI

Nothing says Italy like *caffè* does. While cuisine changes from city to city, and region to region, coffee is the common thread that brings all Italians together. That's not to say all coffees are equal, or that it isn't the basis for rigorous debate, but if there's one thing Italians can agree on it's *il caffè*. They argue over soccer, politics and how many eggs go into making the perfect *carbonara*, but when it comes to coffee, they're suddenly all on the same page. It is an age-old and sacred ritual they will defend until their death.

Romans prepare their coffee at home with the classic moka percolator (or *caffettiera* as it's referred to by Italians around the world), and at the bar, coffee comes in all shapes and sizes. There's *cappuccino*, short, long, *macchiato* with hot milk, *macchiato* with cold milk and the list goes on. In summer, there are even more to choose from: *cappuccino freddo*, *macchiato freddo* and the famous Roman *grattachecca*. The *grattachecca* is a hand-shaved ice drink, served with your choice of flavoured syrup. The coffee version is similar to a *granita* and comes served with *panna* (cream). Refreshing during the stifling Roman summer, they are served at street stands across the city, including a couple of famous ones along the Tiber River.

Angelo Severini is the bar manager and barista at the Rome Cavalieri, Waldorf Astoria Hotel, and knows a thing or two about coffee. He says that for Italians, drinking coffee is like a religious ritual, yet one that takes place at any time of day. 'Italian coffee is always *espresso* and we drink it in a ceramic coffee cup or a glass.'

My local bar — because every single Italian has one — represents the sights, smells and sounds of Italy. If I stand at the counter and close my eyes, I hear the coffee machine spurting, cups and saucers clapping and I can smell that strong aroma. You have your coffee and breakfast standing right there at the bar (there's an additional cost applied to table service). Italian breakfast isn't bacon and eggs, but coffee and a *cornetto* (Italy's version of a croissant). It's also a meeting point, like the *piazza* in a way. But coffee time isn't about lingering as you would over an afternoon tea or brunch; you drink your coffee like a shot, say your hellos and goodbyes and you're off.

Italians start the day with coffee, and it's rare to end a meal without one. The dining process in Italy follows a sequence. After you've eaten, you might have dessert, but never coffee and dessert together. You order your coffee last. But then comes one more thing, the *digestivo* or *amaro*. This is a digestive liqueur or *amaro*, the Italian word for bitter, because that's usually what they are. On the Amalfi Coast you might end your meal with a *limoncello* or in Sicily a *passito* (sweet fortified wine, similar to port). In Rome, you have an *amaro* or even a *grappa* (an Italian style of brandy). They are all said to contain medicinal properties and Italians strongly believe they aid the digestion process.

I actually don't drink coffee or *amaro*. There, I said it. (I don't drink beer, either, for that matter, so as an Italian-Australian, I'm a national shame in two countries!) So for me, the bar experience can get a little awkward when I'm invited in by a friend or colleague. I learnt very early on that tea was not an option; nobody has time for that drawn-out process at the bar. I eventually opted for the freshly squeezed juice that is available at just about every single bar in Italy, and is another reason I love this country so much.

Given the reverence Italians have for their coffee and *digestivi*, you can imagine my embarrassment at the first dinner party I hosted for Roman friends, when at the end of the meal they all seemed to be sitting around waiting for something. I'd forgotten the coffee and *amaro* and they've never let me live it down! It was a rookie mistake I made sure to never commit again.

CASTAGNOLE CON CREMA

BY ANTICO FORNO ROSCIOLI

MAKES ABOUT 20

vegetable oil, for frying

butter, for greasing

icing (confectioners') sugar, for dusting

Dough

250 ml (8½ fl oz/1 cup) water

75 g (2¾ oz) butter

185 g (6½ oz/1¼ cups) plain (all-purpose) flour

5 eggs

Pastry cream

4 egg yolks

100 g (3½ oz) sugar

20 g (¾ oz) cornflour (cornstarch)

200 ml (7 fl oz) milk

50 ml (1¾ fl oz) fresh cream

½ vanilla bean

zest of ¼ orange, cut into thick strips

To make the dough, heat the water in a saucepan over medium–low heat, add the butter and let it melt into the water. As soon as the mixture starts to boil, remove from the heat, add the flour and beat well using a whisk.

Place the pan back over the heat and cook for another 5 minutes, stirring until a dough forms that easily comes away from the side of the pan.

Remove from the heat and let the mixture cool until it is tepid, then transfer to the bowl of an electric stand mixer. Beat gently, gradually adding in the eggs and a pinch of salt until the mixture is smooth and elastic.

Heat plenty of vegetable oil in a large heavy-based saucepan until boiling — about 180°C (350°F) on a cooking thermometer.

While the oil is heating, transfer the dough mixture to a piping (icing) bag. Grease a sheet of baking paper with butter, then pipe the dough onto the paper, into rounds about 5 cm (2 inches) in diameter. Cut the paper around the dough, then one by one slide the dough rounds into the boiling oil — the paper should slide away easily after a few seconds over the heat. Working in batches, fry them for a minute or two until golden; they should puff up as soon as they hit the hot oil. Drain on paper towel and leave to cool.

While the *castagnole* are cooling, make the pastry cream by beating the egg yolks and sugar together until creamy. Gradually add the cornflour and a little of the milk and mix until you have a smooth paste. Set aside.

Pour the rest of the milk and the cream into a saucepan. Cut the vanilla bean in half lengthways, then use a teaspoon to scrape the seeds from one half into the pan and add the scraped bean as well. Add the orange zest. Gently bring to the boil, then strain to remove the vanilla bean and orange zest.

Return the infused milk to the pan and add the beaten egg yolk mixture. Stir well over medium heat for about 4–5 minutes, or until the custard starts to thicken. When it is dense and smooth, remove from the heat and leave to cool, covered with plastic wrap.

Transfer the cooled pastry cream to a clean piping bag. Poke a hole in the *castagnole* and pipe the pastry cream inside them. Dust with icing sugar and serve.

Castagnole are best enjoyed straight away, before they become soggy. Otherwise sprinkle again with icing sugar right before serving to freshen them up, as they do in Roman *pasticcerie*.

This version of these custard-filled, sugar-coated fried doughnuts is from Antico Forno Roscioli, where during *Carnevale* you'll see small crowds of Romans eating them on the street just out front. In Rome, you can buy these pre-cooked at the *pasticceria*, but they aren't all that difficult to make at home.

Let them cool before filling with your *crema*, and dust them generously with icing sugar before serving.

Gina Tringali is a successful Italian-American food and travel writer based in Rome, and is co-owner of tour operator Casa Mia Italy Food & Wine. So yes, she knows her food and wine! For Gina, this recipe evokes strong family food memories. Her family background has ties to Naples, and she would make these in her *nonna's* kitchen on the feast day of San Giuseppe (Saint Joseph), which is Father's Day in Italy.

Filled with custard, these divine doughnuts are traditionally served with a few sour or black cherries on top, and a generous dusting of icing sugar. They can be baked, but I can never go past the fried ones.

Despite being more traditionally Neapolitan, around Father's Day and *Carnevale* you will also find these in Rome, alongside the Roman version, *bignè*.

ZEPPOLE DI SAN GIUSEPPE

BY GINA TRINGALI

MAKES ABOUT 16–20
SERVES 8–10

---

vegetable oil, for frying

---

80 g (2¾ oz) black cherries
in syrup

---

icing (confectioners')
sugar, for dusting

PASTRY CREAM

---

500 ml (17 fl oz/2 cups)
milk

---

zest of 1 lemon, cut into
large strips

---

4 eggs

---

180 g (6½ oz) sugar

---

75 g (2¾ oz/½ cup) plain
(all-purpose) flour

Dough

---

350 ml (12 fl oz) water

---

1 tablespoon sugar

---

80 g (2¾ oz) butter, cubed

---

1 tablespoon brandy

---

185 g (6½ oz/1¼ cups) plain
(all-purpose) flour

---

5 eggs

To make the pastry cream, bring the milk to the boil in a saucepan. Add the lemon zest strips, remove from the heat, then cover and set aside to infuse for at least 30 minutes.

In a bowl, whisk together the eggs and sugar, then gradually add the flour, mixing well. Add the mixture to the infused milk and bring back to the boil, stirring continuously until the ingredients are combined and the mixture is thick and smooth. Remove the lemon zest strips and leave to cool.

To make the dough, combine the water, sugar, butter, brandy and a pinch of salt in a saucepan. Heat and bring to the boil, mixing continuously with a wooden spoon or whisk.

Remove from the heat and add the flour. Mix until the flour is combined, then place the pan back over medium–low heat and stir for about 5 minutes, until it is smooth and comes away from the side of the pan.

Remove from the heat and let the mixture cool. Once cooled, add the eggs, one at a time, mixing to form a soft dough.

Heat plenty of vegetable oil in a deep heavy-based saucepan until boiling — about 180°C (350°F) on a cooking thermometer.

While the oil is heating, place the dough in a piping (icing) bag fitted with a 12–14 mm (½ inch) star-shaped nozzle. Cut some baking paper into 16–20 individual 10 cm (4 inch) squares, then pipe the dough onto the paper squares in a doughnut-ring shape.

Carefully slide the dough and paper into the hot oil two at a time, to avoid overcrowding the pan. As the dough begins to fry, the paper will come away and you can remove it with a slotted spoon. Cook the *zeppole* on each side for about 3 minutes, or until golden and puffed.

Drain on paper towel and leave to cool while cooking the remaining *zeppole*. Leave to cool completely.

Pipe the cooled pastry cream into the middle of each *zeppole*. Top each with two or three cherries and sprinkle with icing sugar.

The *zeppole* are best enjoyed straight away, but will keep in an airtight container in the fridge for a day or so.

BIGNÈ DI SAN GIUSEPPE

BY GINA TRINGALI

SERVES 6

vegetable oil, for frying

icing (confectioners') sugar, for dusting

Dough

250 ml (8½ fl oz/1 cup) water

60 g (2 oz) butter

120 g (4½ oz) plain (all-purpose) flour

3 eggs, plus 1 egg yolk

1 tablespoon sugar

finely grated zest of ½ lemon

Pastry cream

500 ml (17 fl oz/2 cups) milk

zest of 1 lemon, cut into large strips

4 eggs

180 g (6½ oz) sugar

75 g (2¾ oz/½ cup) plain (all-purpose) flour

To make the dough, put the water, butter and a pinch of salt in a saucepan and bring to the boil over medium heat. As soon as the mixture begins to boil, remove it from the heat, then add the flour and beat with a whisk until smooth.

Place the pan back over the heat. Stir continuously, keeping the mixture from boiling again, until the mixture comes away from the side of the pan. Remove from the heat and leave to cool.

When the mixture has cooled, add the eggs, one at a time, then the egg yolk, mixing continuously until they are well incorporated into the dough. Then add the sugar and lemon zest, mixing well; the dough will be quite sticky. Wrap the dough in a clean tea towel and leave to rest for 30 minutes.

While the dough is resting, make the pastry cream. Bring the milk to the boil in a saucepan. Add the lemon zest strips, remove from the heat, then cover and set aside to infuse.

In a bowl, whisk together the eggs and sugar, then gradually add the flour, mixing well. Add the mixture to the infused milk and bring back to the boil, stirring continuously until the ingredients are combined and the mixture is creamy. Remove the lemon zest strips and set aside to cool.

When you are ready to fry the *bignè*, heat plenty of vegetable oil in a large heavy-based saucepan until just boiling — about 170°C (340°F) on a cooking thermometer.

Take a spoonful of the dough mixture and use a second spoon to mould it into a ball shape, before carefully dropping it into the hot oil; the *bignè* will puff up as soon as it hits the oil. Continue adding more *bignè* until the pan is full, but not overcrowded. Cook for 2–3 minutes, or until golden, gently rotating them with a slotted spoon to ensure an even colour, then remove from the oil and drain on paper towel. Continue until all the *bignè* have been fried, and leave them to cool completely.

Fill a piping (icing) bag with the cooled pastry cream. Poke a hole in the *bignè* and pipe the pastry cream inside them. Dust with icing sugar and serve.

The *bignè* are best enjoyed straight away, but will keep in an airtight container in the fridge for a day or so.

Bignè are the Roman version of the Neapolitan *zeppole*. While *zeppole* are doughnut-shaped, *bignè* are round, similar to large profiteroles. They can be baked or fried, and like *zeppole* are filled with delicious custard cream. Not surprisingly, every Italian has a slightly different version, Gina tells me.

Romans often make these at home for Father's Day, but don't restrict yourself to one day a year, because they are to die for.

A CAS

Many food experts or people in Italy will tell you that the main influence for cuisine from north to south comes from the market or the farm. Well, they're wrong. Italian food customs and traditions are born in the home — *a casa*. Empires and political regimes have collapsed around Rome, but the one thing that remains sacred (aside from soccer perhaps, and in Rome there's only one team by the way), is the family structure.

Mothers and grandmothers are particularly revered by Italians, by both men and women alike, and are the moral compasses of the family. More often than not, when you ask a Roman where to eat in Rome they will say, *a casa di mamma* or *a casa di nonna* (mum or grandma's house).

Growing up in an Italian family, my earliest memories of my mum are also at home in the kitchen. Born in Abruzzo, as a young girl she was taught by my *nonna* how to make egg pasta at home in Australia. As a child, I remember her bringing out the large wooden board to make *gnocchi* and *ravioloni* (large *ravioli*; you'd fit only two or three on a plate). On the stove a big pot of *ragù* would sit to bubble away for hours. She'd put it on a low heat and ask me to watch the sauce as she did other household chores.

Her *brodo di gallina* (chicken broth) warmed the heart and soothed you when you were sick. *Brodo con stracciatella* is an egg-drop soup, where you pour an egg and cheese

mixture into your boiling broth and as it cooks it breaks up into little pieces (*stracciare* is the Italian verb for 'rip' or 'shred'). On special occasions, especially during *le feste* (celebrations like Easter and Christmas), as her mother and her own *nonna* did, Mum adds tiny meatballs, pieces of chicken that have slow-cooked in the broth and tiny homemade croutons to the *brodo*. To this day, I make the exact same dish, the precise way she taught me, and that's now at least four generations strong.

Recipes like these have been kept alive for centuries and, in cases such as mine, have transcended continents with migration. Food traditions never die in Italy because they are intrinsically linked to family memories. And the appreciation that Italians have for quality, yet simple, food, and the pride that comes with that, is unrivalled anywhere in the world.

Even in modern Italy, where fewer young people are cooking at home and there is rigorous debate around the preservation of culinary heritage, tradition still seems to prevail. In fact, the dishes of yesteryear continue to appear on restaurant menus, and ones that were predominantly reserved for the home have even made a fashionable comeback.

Together with the homemade *ravioloni* my mum would make and *pizzelle* (Abruzzese-style waffles), *brodo con stracciatella* is the most heartwarming food memory of my childhood. I didn't even know it had an English title because in our household, this egg-drop soup was just *brodo* (the Italian word for 'broth'). My *nonna*, then my mother, and now I, make it with chicken, but *manzo* (beef) is also common in Italy, although you could very well leave the meat out altogether.

In my family, *brodo con stracciatella* was historically on the menu for special occasions (even at Christmas, under the hot Australian summer sun!), but as time went on, it became a winter staple, and comfort food for when one of us kids were sick or came home after a long trip.

Small egg pasta, *quadrucci* or *tortellini* can also be added to the broth at the final stage and cooked until *al dente*, before adding the egg.

BRODO DI MAMMA CON STRACCIATELLA

(Mum's chicken and egg-drop soup)

BY LINA PASQUALE

**SERVES 4;
MAKES 2 LITRES
(68 FL OZ/8 CUPS)
OF BROTH**

Broth

200 g (7 oz) boneless
chicken breast (with or
without skin)

160 g (5½ oz) chicken thigh
(with or without skin)

1 large carrot, halved

1 onion, halved

2 celery stalks, with leaves

150 g (5½ oz) tinned
chopped tomatoes

Stracciatella

1 egg

3 tablespoons grated
Parmigiano Reggiano

To make the broth, place the chicken pieces in a large saucepan, add the carrot, onion and celery and cover with 3 litres (101 fl oz/12 cups) cold water. Add the tomatoes and season with salt.

Bring the pan to the boil, using a ladle to skim off any foam that develops on the surface. Cover the broth and leave to boil for 1 hour over high heat. Reduce the heat to low and simmer for a further 1 hour, then remove from the heat and leave to cool completely.

Remove the chicken and vegetables using a slotted spoon and set aside. Finely strain the broth through a sieve until clear, then pour it back into the saucepan.

Slice the boiled chicken and divide among four bowls; the leftover vegetables can be kept and used in a vegetable soup.

Beat the egg in a small bowl, then add the parmigiano and a pinch of salt and mix together well.

Bring the broth back to the boil, pour in the egg mixture, stir quickly and turn off the heat. Ladle the broth over the chicken and serve hot.

PASTA ALL'UOVO

(Fresh egg pasta)

BY CARLA TOMASI

Nothing warms my heart more than the childhood memories I have of my mother making homemade pasta. You knew lunch or dinner was going to be special when the big wooden board and the pasta machine came out. Mum would make *tagliatelle* and large *ravioli* filled with *ricotta* and meat. You would only serve two or three per plate, and they were to die for.

For this recipe, I went to Carla Tomasi, who is renowned in Rome for her divine pasta-making skills. Her *pasta all'uovo* is extra silky-smooth and is sure to become a staple in your home for years to come. While pasta-making requires some practice and technique, it's not difficult or time consuming, so don't be put off by the thought. Instead, roll your sleeves up and enjoy the satisfaction of your very own homemade *pasta all'uovo*!

SERVES 4

4 eggs, at room
temperature

600 g (1 lb 5 oz/4 cups) '00'
flour, plus extra for dusting

Break the eggs into a bowl and weigh them. Beat lightly with a fork, then add almost double the weight of flour.

Using a fork, or your fingertips, gradually work the eggs into the flour. Once lightly mixed, turn the dough onto a clean worktop or large wooden chopping board and begin kneading, using the heel of your hand to push down on the mixture. Your kneading, along with the heat from your hands, should begin to turn the dough silky smooth.

Once the dough is soft, leave it to rest under an upturned mixing bowl in a cool place for at least 15 minutes. (At this point, the dough can be refrigerated until the following day and slowly brought back to room temperature before use.)

Once rested, the dough can be rolled out into sheets. Divide the dough into four portions and work on one piece at a time, leaving the others covered with a tea towel (dish towel) or plastic wrap.

Clamp your pasta machine to a work surface and set the dial to the widest setting. Flatten the piece of dough so it will fit through the machine, then pass it through the rollers. Fold the dough like an envelope and pass it through again. If the dough feels sticky, dust it with a little flour to dry the surface. Repeat this process five or six times; the result should be a smooth piece of dough almost the width of the rollers.

To begin stretching the dough, set the dial of the machine down one notch and roll again. Continue reducing the thickness and rolling once, until the dough is thin and stretchy. There is no need to fold the dough again, but once the length exceeds 25 cm (10 inches), cut it in half and work in separate, shorter pieces. Dust with flour whenever the dough begins to feel tacky. If the pasta develops holes as you roll, check that there are no residual pieces of dough under the rollers causing it to tear.

Once you are happy with the thickness of the pasta, lay it out to dry on tea towels sprinkled with flour.

Repeat the process with the other pieces of dough, until it is all rolled out to the same thickness.

Leave the pasta sheets to dry out for at least 20 minutes in a cool place away from sunlight, turning them over three or four times. The sheets are ready for cutting when the dough is still pliable, but fairly dry to the touch; test by cutting a small piece into strands — if they stick together, wait a little longer.

Cut the pasta into the desired shape with a sharp knife, or use the setting for *tagliatelle* or *tagliolini* on your pasta machine and roll the dough through. If you have too much pasta, it can be left to dry fully and then stored in an airtight container in a cool place for up to 3 months, or in the refrigerator for 5 days.

Cook the fresh pasta in a large saucepan of boiling salted water for about 2–3 minutes, or until *al dente,* and serve with your chosen sauce.

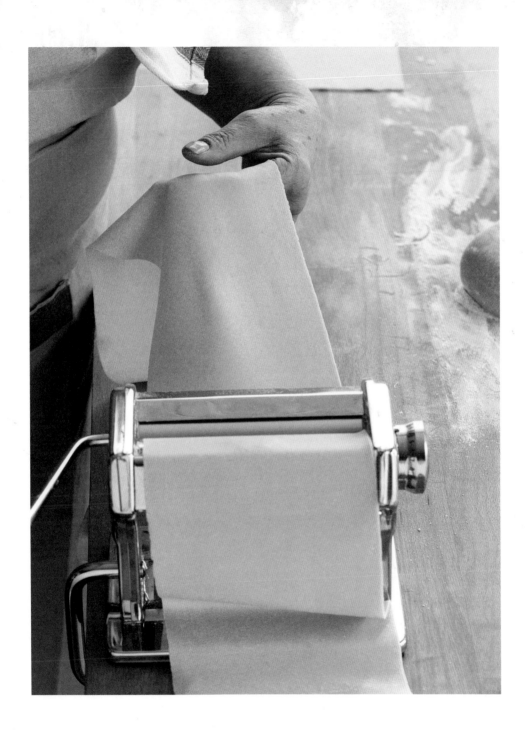

SUGO DI POMODORO

(Quick tomato sauce)

BY CARLA TOMASI

SERVES 4

90 ml (3 fl oz) extra virgin olive oil

600 g (1 lb 5 oz) cherry tomatoes, halved

10 g (¼ oz) unsalted butter (optional)

3 tablespoons shredded basil leaves

This simple tomato sauce, also by Carla, is the classic Italian accompaniment to homemade pasta because it is simple and light. You can serve your pasta with your sauce of choice, but remember to keep it simple — egg pasta is rich and shouldn't be matched with equally rich sauces, or its flavour will get lost.

This sauce is quick and easy to prepare, and will no doubt become a favourite in your home too.

Heat the olive oil in a large, lidded frying pan over high heat. Add the tomatoes and quickly cover with the lid. Holding the lid in place, shake the pan back and forth to caramelise the sugar in the tomatoes.

Remove the lid and cook for a further 1–2 minutes, then season with salt and freshly ground black pepper.

To use, cook your chosen pasta until *al dente*, drain, then add to the tomatoes with 3 tablespoons of the pasta water and the butter, if using.

Toss the pasta in the sauce, and once the butter has melted, add the basil and serve.

GNOCCHETTI CON POMODORO E TRIGLIA

(Gnocchi with tomato and red mullet)

BY CRISTINA BOWERMAN

SERVES 4–6

2 tablespoons extra virgin olive oil

1 garlic clove, peeled

1 small onion, finely chopped

500 g (1 lb 2 oz) San Marzano or cherry tomatoes, crushed

800 g (1 lb 12 oz) red mullet fillets; if not available, you could use bream, dory, garfish, snapper or whiting

fresh basil, microgreens or salad leaves, to garnish

Fish stock

1 kg (2 lb 3 oz) fish bones

Gnocchetti

250 g (9 oz) floury/boiling potatoes

80 g (2¾ oz) plain (all-purpose) flour, plus extra for dusting

50 g (1¾ oz) cornflour (cornstarch) or potato starch

½ teaspoon salt

To make the stock, place the fish bones in a saucepan and cover with 2 litres (68 fl oz/8 cups) cold water. Bring to the boil, then turn down the heat, cover and simmer for 40 minutes. Strain and set aside.

Meanwhile, make the *gnocchetti*. Put the potatoes, whole and with the skins on, in a large saucepan. Cover with cold water and add a pinch of salt. Boil for 30–40 minutes, or until just soft, then drain and leave until cool enough to handle. Peel off the skins, then mash roughly in a bowl, or pass them through a potato ricer.

Sift the flour, cornflour and salt into the bowl of mashed potato and bring the ingredients together using a fork. Once the mixture resembles large breadcrumbs, use your hands to knead the dough on the bench until soft and smooth — if the dough is too dry, add a splash of water; if it is too wet, add a little more flour.

Cut off a piece of the dough and, using your fingertips, roll it into a sausage shape about the same diameter as your finger. Cut into pieces about 2 cm (¾ inch) long, then roll each piece into a ball to form the *gnocchetti*. Place on a lightly floured surface and continue until all of the dough has been used.

The *gnocchetti* can be refrigerated for a few hours before using, should you wish to make them in advance.

To make the sauce, heat the olive oil in a large frying pan. Add the whole garlic clove and cook over medium heat until it starts to sizzle, then remove. Add the onion and cook gently for 5 minutes, until translucent.

Add the tomatoes and a couple of ladlefuls of the fish broth. Stir together and leave to simmer, uncovered, for 15–20 minutes, adding a little more fish stock if necessary if the mixture starts to dry up or get too thick. Season with salt and freshly ground black pepper to taste. If you prefer a smoother sauce, you can blend it using a hand-held stick blender, or alternatively leave it a little chunkier.

Add the fish fillets to the sauce and cook for another 5 minutes to poach the fish.

Meanwhile, bring a large saucepan of salted water to the boil. Add the *gnocchetti* and cook for 1–2 minutes, until they rise to the surface. Remove the *gnocchetti* using a slotted spoon and place into the pan with the sauce. Mix to coat in the sauce.

Serve with the fish fillets arranged on top, and a garnish of shredded basil, microgreens or salad leaves.

In my first months in Rome I lived in apartments on two historic Trastevere streets — Vicolo del Bologna and Vicolo de Cinque. These are the streets that come up on your online image search for beautiful Trastevere because they are narrow, have Roman-coloured buildings and a vintage Fiat 500 is never far away. Where these streets intersect, you'll find Glass Hostaria by Cristina Bowerman, the only female Michelin-star chef in Rome, and my friend. This is her recipe — a refined instalment of your usual *gnocchi* for when you want to impress. They are *gnocchetti,* which means they are smaller than *gnocchi* and round in shape.

Cristina recommends this light tomato sauce with red mullet, but you could of course serve with a sauce of your choosing.

SPAGHETTI AJO, OJO E PEPERONCINO

(Spaghetti with garlic, oil and chilli)

BY ANGELO PREZIOSI

SERVES 4

400 g (14 oz) spaghetti

150 ml (5 fl oz) extra virgin olive oil

2 garlic cloves, thinly sliced

2 red chillies, seeded and finely chopped

1 small bunch of Italian (flat-leaf) parsley, chopped

Spaghettata is the term for a feast of *spaghetti*, always for more than one, and often made at home. As a child, when family parties went late, after midnight — and it didn't matter how much you'd eaten prior — someone would put the water on the boil to make a quick pasta. In my family, it was *spaghetti con alici* (spaghetti with anchovies), and in Angelo's it was always this one: spaghetti with garlic, oil and chilli. He says it's the Italian version of a late-night, post-drinking kebab, and he's whipped up many a one at 2am!

Bring a large saucepan of salted water to the boil. Add the pasta and cook for the time indicated on the packet.

Meanwhile, gently heat the olive oil in a frying pan and add the garlic. Cook over medium heat for a minute or two until the garlic begins to soften, then add the chilli and season with a little salt. Cook for a further minute to infuse the oil, then turn off the heat so the garlic doesn't burn.

When the pasta is *al dente*, drain it and add to the frying pan with a few spoonfuls of the cooking water. Cook over medium heat for a couple of minutes, adding the parsley and stirring together well to coat the pasta in the oil.

Serve immediately.

MINESTRA DI BROCCOLI E ARZILLA

(Skate and broccoli soup)

BY DOMENICO STILE, ENOTECA LA TORRE

SERVES 6

3 tablespoons extra virgin olive oil

2 garlic cloves, peeled

1 small red chilli, seeded

4 anchovy fillets in olive oil

200 g (7 oz) tinned chopped tomatoes

60 ml (2 fl oz/¼ cup) dry white wine

1 Romanesco broccoli

200 g (7 oz) spaghetti

Fish stock

1 skate, weighing about 1 kg (2 lb 3 oz)

1 onion

1 carrot

1 celery stalk

6 Italian (flat-leaf) parsley sprigs

To make the stock, rinse the skate under running water, place in a large saucepan and cover with 2 litres (68 fl oz/8 cups) cold water. Cut the onion, carrot and celery in half and add to the pan with the parsley stalks (keeping aside the leaves). Season well with salt, cover and bring to the boil, then reduce the heat to low and cook for 15 minutes.

Use a slotted spoon to remove the skate from the broth and separate the fillets. Discard the head, skin and gristle, then put the remaining bones back into the broth, along with any juices. Cover and continue to cook for a further 30 minutes. The skate fillets can be set aside and used for a starter or main course.

Heat the olive oil in another large saucepan finely chop the garlic, chilli and reserved parsley leaves. Add them to the oil and cook for a few minutes over medium heat, until just beginning to soften. Add the anchovies and cook for another 3 minutes, pushing them down with the back of a fork to dissolve them in the oil. Add the tomatoes and wine, stir everything together, then cover and continue to cook for 15 minutes.

Divide the broccoli into small florets, cutting the larger ones in half if necessary. Add the broccoli to the pan, turn the heat up and cook for 3–4 minutes in the tomato sauce.

Strain the fish stock through a fine-meshed sieve, then pour into the pan of broccoli and tomatoes. Add any extra pieces of fish from the strained leftovers. Mix well, then leave to boil together for 10 minutes.

Break the spaghetti into lengths of about 2 cm (¾ inch) and add them to the soup. Leave to boil for another 10 minutes, or until the spaghetti is *al dente*.

Serve immediately.

This humble soup of *Romanesco broccoli* and skate fish was traditionally eaten on Christmas Eve. Thickened with *spaghetti*, it is a hearty meal in itself, prepared commonly in the home, but making somewhat of a comeback on some *trattoria* menus. Ask your fishmonger to clean and remove the skin from your skate fillets, but leave the bones in to give the soup more flavour. A better substitute for Roman broccoli is cauliflower, as opposed to regular broccoli.

This is chef Domenico Stile's version. At 28, he is impressively Rome's youngest Michelin-star chef and manages the talented team at Enoteca La Torre, which sits within a stunning Art Deco building owned by Roman fashion house, Fendi.

Simple, cheap and good for you, on cold winter nights nothing is heartier than pasta with chickpeas. Quintessentially Roman, it's the *cucina povera* of central Italy. It is customary to use a mix of small pasta; the idea was to use up whatever sort you had in your pantry.

My beautiful Roman friend Fernanda made this version for me one night, and for me, hers is perfect, so I was hell-bent on including it here. The rosemary and sage give just the right herby hint to the nutty chickpeas. Fernanda usually makes it with *pancetta*, which adds a nice salty kick, but this is optional.

Another trick she learnt from her mother, Anna, is to add some of the juices of a roast (whether chicken, beef, lamb, whatever) you may have cooked that day or the day before. Again, this is optional, but it sure does enhance the flavour.

PASTA E CECI
(Pasta and chickpeas)

BY FERNANDA MENOZZI

SERVES 4–6

60 ml (2 fl oz/¼ cup) extra virgin olive oil

1 golden (French) shallot, finely chopped

1 garlic clove, peeled

1 small carrot, finely diced

½ celery stalk, finely diced

1 rosemary sprig

100 g (3½ oz) smoked pancetta, diced (optional)

60 ml (2 fl oz/¼ cup) dry white wine

150 g (5½ oz) fresh cherry tomatoes, chopped (or you can use tinned chopped tomatoes)

250 g (9 oz) dried chickpeas, soaked in water for 12 hours (or 500 g/ 1 lb 2 oz cooked chickpeas)

1 tablespoon chopped sage

1 tablespoon chopped rosemary

250 g (9 oz) mixed small pasta

Heat the olive oil in a large saucepan and add the shallot and whole garlic clove. Gently fry over medium–low heat for about 5 minutes, until the shallot is soft, then remove the garlic.

Add the carrot, celery, rosemary sprig and pancetta, if using, and cook for 2–3 minutes. Pour in the wine and leave to simmer for another 2 minutes, or until the alcohol evaporates.

Stir in the tomatoes and continue to cook over a low heat for 10 minutes. Add the drained soaked chickpeas and 1 litre (34 fl oz/ 4 cups) water. Bring to the boil, then turn down the heat and simmer for 2 hours, adding a little water occasionally if it becomes too dry. (If using cooked chickpeas, add them at same point, but cook for only 1–1½ hours.)

About 30 minutes before the end of cooking, add the sage and rosemary, and season with salt and freshly ground black pepper to taste.

When the chickpeas are soft, bring the pan back to the boil. Add the pasta and, if necessary, another glass of water to enable the pasta to cook. Cook for 5 minutes, then turn off the heat and cover the pan; the pasta will continue to cook in the residual heat.

Leave for 10 minutes, then serve.

POLLO CON I PEPERONI

(Chicken with peppers)

BY ANGELO PREZIOSI

SERVES 4

100 ml (3½ fl oz) extra
virgin olive oil

1.2 kg (2 lb 10 oz) chicken
thighs and legs, on the bone

2 yellow capsicums
(bell peppers)

2 red capsicums
(bell peppers)

125 ml (4 fl oz/½ cup)
dry white wine

400 g (14 oz) tin chopped
tomatoes

Heat the olive oil in a large saucepan. Add the chicken pieces,
season with salt and freshly ground black pepper and cook over
high heat for 10–15 minutes, turning regularly to brown on all sides.

Meanwhile, remove the stems and seeds from the capsicums,
then cut the capsicums into chunky strips measuring roughly
4 x 2 cm (1¼ x ¾ inch).

Add the wine to the chicken and leave to simmer for a few minutes
to evaporate the alcohol. Add the capsicum strips and cook for
5 minutes, then add the tomatoes and 500 ml (17 fl oz/2 cups) water.

Season with a little more salt and pepper, stir well and cook over
medium–low heat for 45 minutes, or up to 1 hour. If the sauce begins
to dry out too much during cooking, stir in a little more water.

The dish is ready to serve when the chicken is tender (the meat
will easily come away from the bone) and the capsicum is soft.

Serve with some bread if you like, to mop up the sauces.

Pollo con i peperoni, also known as *pollo alla Romana* (Roman-style chicken), is a popular *trattoria* dish that is still often cooked in Roman households. Angelo's recipe is quite precious, in being at least three generations old, with his *nonna* Rosa passing it down to his mother Cristina, and then to him.

It's a dish that takes no time to prepare, and it's roast chicken at its best: slow-cooked with sweet and sticky capsicums. Angelo says it's also amazing in a sandwich the next day.

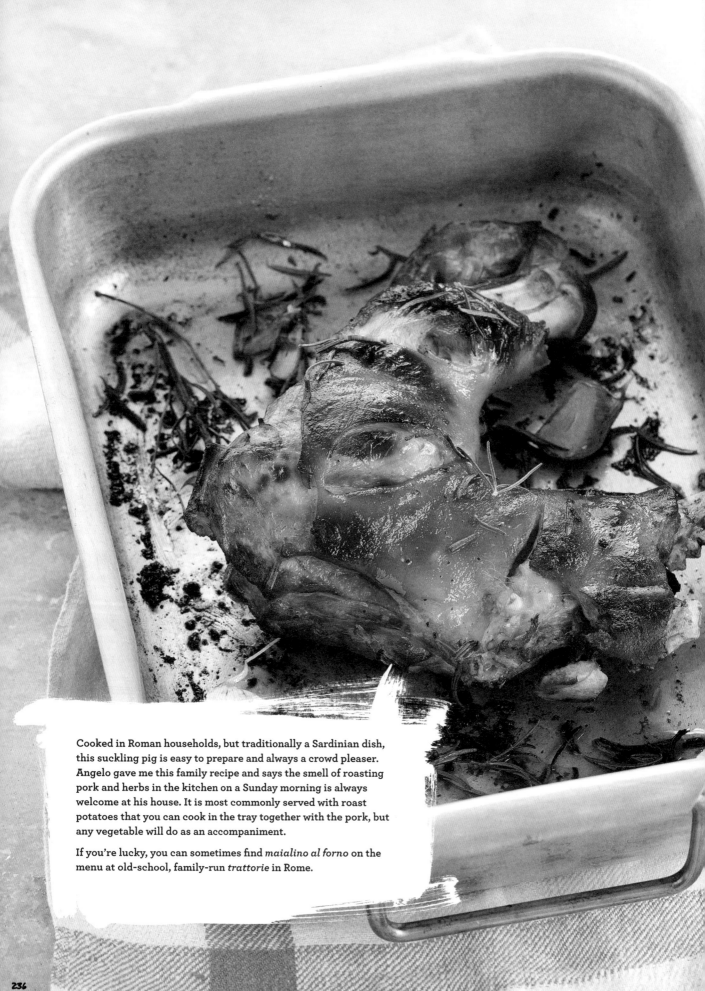

Cooked in Roman households, but traditionally a Sardinian dish, this suckling pig is easy to prepare and always a crowd pleaser. Angelo gave me this family recipe and says the smell of roasting pork and herbs in the kitchen on a Sunday morning is always welcome at his house. It is most commonly served with roast potatoes that you can cook in the tray together with the pork, but any vegetable will do as an accompaniment.

If you're lucky, you can sometimes find *maialino al forno* on the menu at old-school, family-run *trattorie* in Rome.

MAIALINO AL FORNO

(Roast suckling pig)

BY ANGELO PREZIOSI

SERVES 4

1 whole garlic bulb

10 rosemary sprigs

3 tablespoons extra virgin olive oil

2 kg (4 lb 6 oz) suckling pig

Preheat the oven to 170°C (340°F).

Cut the garlic bulb in half, leaving the skin on, and place in a large roasting tin, along with the rosemary sprigs.

Rub the olive oil all over the pork using your hands, and season well with salt and freshly ground black pepper. Place the pork in the roasting tin, on top of the rosemary and garlic, skin side down.

Bake for 1 hour, then turn the pork over and roast for a further 20 minutes. The skin should be crispy and the meat tender and juicy.

Carve into pieces and serve.

POLPETTE DI BOLLITO

(Fried meatballs)

BY MAURIZIO MISSO

SERVES 4

2 eggs

400 g (14 oz) fine dry breadcrumbs

vegetable oil, for frying

Meatballs

1 x 500 g (1 lb 2 oz) piece of beef for boiling (such as brisket)

1 onion, quartered

1 small carrot, halved

1 celery stalk, halved

2 cloves

1 small whole chicken

2 small potatoes

2 slices of white bread

150 ml (5 fl oz) milk

150 g (5½ oz) mortadella, finely chopped

1 garlic clove, crushed and finely chopped

10 capers, finely chopped

grated zest of ½ lemon

3 tablespoons chopped Italian (flat-leaf) parsley

2 eggs

80 g (2¾ oz) Parmigiano Reggiano, grated

1 teaspoon freshly grated nutmeg

To make the meatballs, put the beef in a large saucepan, along with the onion, carrot, celery and cloves. Cover with water, bring to the boil, then cover and leave to cook at a rapid boil for 1 hour.

Cut the chicken into large pieces, add to the pan and continue to cook for a further 1 hour.

Meanwhile, put the whole unpeeled potatoes in a separate saucepan, cover with cold water and add a pinch of salt. Bring to the boil, then cook for 25–30 minutes, or until tender. Drain and leave to cool, then remove the skins and mash to a rough purée.

Once the meat has boiled, remove the beef and chicken pieces from the stock and leave to cool. Remove the crusts from the bread and place in a bowl with the milk to soak.

Skin the chicken, and remove the meat from the bones. Finely chop the chicken, along with the beef, and place in a large bowl. Add the mashed potato, mortadella, garlic, capers, lemon zest and parsley and mix together. Beat the eggs, then add to the mixture with the grated parmigiano, nutmeg and a good pinch of salt.

Squeeze the bread to remove any excess milk, then add to the mixture as well. Using your hands, knead everything together until all the ingredients are evenly distributed.

Prepare the coating ingredients by beating the other two eggs in a bowl, and pouring the breadcrumbs into a separate bowl.

Take about 2 tablespoons of the meat mixture and use your hands to shape into a circular patty shape. Coat it in the beaten egg, then in the breadcrumbs, using your hands to evenly pat down the coating. Place on a tray lined with baking paper. Shape and coat the remaining meatball mixture in the same way.

Heat plenty of vegetable oil in a deep heavy-based frying pan until boiling — about 170°C (340°F) on a cooking thermometer. Cook the meatballs in batches for about 7–8 minutes, or until golden, turning regularly to ensure an even colour on both sides.

Drain on paper towel and serve hot.

These delicious meatballs represent everything I love about Italian cooking; nothing goes to waste, and leftovers can be turned into local delicacies. *Bollito* is the Italian word for 'boiled'. These meatballs are made with the beef and chicken that has been used to make stock, and can commonly be found in Rome, from *trattoria* menus to street food stands.

My Roman-born friend Maurizio Misso makes my favourite ones, and this is his recipe, which has been influenced by his travels and time spent living abroad, as well as his passion for Roman traditions. His love for cooking started at a young age, and he says the tricks he uses in the kitchen have all been stolen from *mamma* and *nonna*!

These *polpette* are seriously addictive. You'll find it hard to stop at just one.

When *polpette al sugo* are on the menu in Rome, I find them hard to resist. They take me back to my childhood, when my mum would have tomato *ragù* on the stove boiling away for hours and often ask me to keep an eye on it. We would eat pasta with the sauce, then have meat and meatballs for seconds.

This version was given to me by one of Rome's most famous restaurants, Roscioli. They serve theirs with *polenta* and shavings of baked *ricotta* for an extra salty hit. Make sure you have some fresh bread handy to mop up that rich tomato sauce.

POLPETTE AL SUGO

(Meatballs and tomato sauce)

BY RISTORANTE SALUMERIA ROSCIOLI

SERVES 4

Meatballs

2 slices of white bread, crusts removed

200 ml (7 fl oz) milk

100 g (3½ oz) mortadella

1 garlic clove

500 g (1 lb 2 oz) minced (ground) beef

250 g (9 oz) minced (ground) pork

250 g (9 oz) minced (ground) veal

grated zest of ½ lemon

1 teaspoon freshly grated nutmeg

140 g (5 oz) Parmigiano Reggiano, grated

1 egg, plus 1 egg yolk, lightly beaten

Sauce

1 kg (2 lb 3 oz) tomatoes

4 golden (French) shallots, finely chopped

100 ml (3½ fl oz) extra virgin olive oil

Start by preparing the meatballs. Soak the bread slices in the milk for 5 minutes. Meanwhile, finely chop the mortadella and garlic, then combine in a large bowl, together with the beef, pork and veal.

Squeeze the excess milk from the bread and add the soaked bread to the meat mixture, along with the lemon zest, nutmeg, parmigiano and beaten egg mixture. Season with salt and freshly ground black pepper and mix well using your hands. Leave to rest while you make the sauce.

Peel the tomatoes by scoring a cross on the bottom of each one, putting them in a heatproof bowl and covering with boiling water. Leave for 30 seconds, then move them to a bowl of cold water and remove the skins by peeling away from the cross. Cut the tomatoes in half and use a spoon to scoop out the seeds, then roughly chop.

Place the chopped tomatoes in a saucepan. Add the shallot, olive oil and a pinch of salt and mix together. Bring to the boil, then simmer over medium–low heat for 20 minutes. Remove from the heat and use a hand-held stick blender to mix the sauce until smooth. Return to the heat and continue to cook for a further 15 minutes.

Meanwhile, using wet hands, shape the meat mixture into balls the size of golf balls; each one should weigh about 70 g (2½ oz).

Once all the meatballs have been formed, and the sauce has cooked for the required time, place them directly into the tomato sauce and leave to poach for 45 minutes, stirring occasionally, until they are cooked through.

Adjust the seasoning and serve immediately with a few spoonfuls of sauce. Any leftover sauce can be served with pasta.

COTECHINO E LENTICCHIE

(Pork sausage and lentils)

BY ANGELO PREZIOSI

SERVES 4

300 g (10½ oz) cotechino
(or 4 pork sausages;
see Note)

60 ml (2 fl oz/¼ cup)
extra virgin olive oil

1 onion, finely diced

1 carrot, finely diced

1 celery stalk, finely diced

1 garlic clove, finely
chopped

3 tablespoons chopped
rosemary

300 g (10½ oz) small brown
dried lentils

750 ml (25½ fl oz/3 cups)
vegetable stock

2 tablespoons tomato paste
(concentrated purée)

Prick the cotechino with a fork, place in a saucepan and cover with cold water. Bring to the boil, then reduce the heat to low and cook for 2 hours. Remove from the water, wrap in foil and set aside until ready to serve.

Heat the olive oil in a large saucepan and gently fry the onion, carrot, celery and garlic for 2 minutes, or until soft.

Add the rosemary and unsoaked lentils. Stir well and cook for 30 seconds, before adding the stock and tomato purée. Season with salt and freshly ground black pepper. Stir well, then simmer, uncovered, over medium–low heat for 45 minutes, stirring occasionally, until the lentils are tender.

Spoon the lentils into four bowls. Unwrap the cotechino, then remove the casing and cut into slices about 1 cm (½ inch) thick. Layer a few pieces of cotechino on top of the lentils and serve.

✳ NOTE: The cotechino can be substituted with 4 pork sausages. Prick the sausages and brown them in the olive oil, before adding the onion, carrot, celery and garlic. Proceed as above, leaving them in the pan until the lentils have finished simmering.

Typically a northern Italian dish, but nowadays eaten all over Italy, this is the customary dish for New Year's Eve. *Cotechino* is a large pork sausage and is traditionally served at this time of year with lentils, which because of their coin shape, represent good fortune and prosperity. In the lead-up to the festive season, butchers and delis across Rome stock *cotechino* to meet the annual New Year's Eve rush.

Angelo's wife and my good friend Kate Zagorski prepares this one at the Preziosi household every year.

"Each, in its own way, was unforgettable.
It would be difficult to — Rome! By all means,
Rome. I will cherish my visit here in memory
as long as I live."

— AUDREY HEPBURN

WHERE TO EAT AND DRINK IN ROME

STREET FOOD

I SUPPLÌ (TRASTEVERE)

Via di San Francesco a Ripa 137
Ph 06 5897110

For the best marinara pizza in Rome, *supplì* and wholesome food on the run.

TRAPIZZINO (TESTACCIO)

Via Giovanni Branca 88
www.trapizzino.it

A favourite Roman snack — a pizza pocket filled with delicious home-cooked combinations. (Various locations)

MERCATO CENTRALE (TERMINI)

Via Giovanni Giolitti 36
www.mercatocentrale.it/roma

A large multi-level food court of sorts, centrally located at Termini station.

MORDI E VAI (TESTACCIO)

Box 15, Testaccio Market
Via Beniamino Franklin 12
www.mordievai.it

The best sandwiches in Rome at this Testaccio Market local hangout.

PIZZA

PIZZERIA AI MARMI (TRASTEVERE)

Viale di Trastevere 53/57
Ph 06 5800919

Sit elbow-to-elbow for one of the most authentic Roman pizza experiences.

PIZZERIA REMO (TESTACCIO)

Piazza di Santa Maria Liberatrice 44
Ph 06 5746270

According to many Romans, the best pizza in Rome.

IVO A TRASTEVERE (TRASTEVERE)

Via di San Francesco a Ripa 158
Ph 06 5817082

A Trastevere neighbourhood favourite for good pizza and lovely atmosphere.

GIULIETTA (TESTACCIO)

Piazza dell'Emporio 28
www.giuliettapizzeria.it

A new *pizzeria* offering Roman and Neapolitan style pizzas with a gourmet twist.

PIZZARIUM (CIPRO)

Via della Meloria 43
www.bonci.it

Gourmet pizza by the slice by one of Rome's famous pizza-makers, Gabriele Bonci.

SBANCO (APPIO SAN GIOVANNI)

Via Siria 1
Ph 06 789318

Stefano Callegari's street food snacks and pizzas rarely disappoint, from classic toppings to the more innovative, such as his carbonara or his *cacio e pepe* instalment.

TRATTORIA & RESTAURANTS

DA ENZO AL 29 (TRASTEVERE)

Via dei Vascellari 29
www.daenzoal29.com

Get the real Roman trattoria experience at this family-run hole-in-the-wall joint.

OSTERIA DER BELLI (TRASTEVERE)

Piazza di Sant'Apollonia 11
Ph 06 5803782

For Sardinian and Roman specialties, especially seafood.

FLAVIO AL VELAVEVODETTO (TESTACCIO)

Via di Monte Testaccio 97
www.ristorantevelavevodetto.it

A local hotspot for Roman fare, built into an ancient Roman dumpsite.

PIANOSTRADA LABORATORIO DI CUCINA (CAMPO DE' FIORI)

Via delle Zoccolette 22
www.pianostrada.com

Women are at the helm of this chic and contemporary all-day dining gem with a stunning garden out back.

ROMEO CHEF & BAKER (TESTACCIO)

Piazza dell'Emporio 28
www.romeo.roma.it

For contemporary all-day restaurant dining, gourmet sandwiches and excellent cocktails.

IL SORPASSO (PRATI)

Via Properzio 31–33
www.sorpasso.info

A Prati hotspot for great food at lunch or dinner, cocktails and all-day snacks.

SECONDO TRADIZIONE (CIPRO)

Via Rialto 39
www.secondotradizione.it

A modern take on the old classics in a stylish *bistrot* format.

ROSCIOLI (CAMPO DE' FIORI)

Via dei Giubbonari 21
www.roscioli.com

Stylish restaurant, wine bar and delicatessen with a focus on prized produce.

CHINAPPI (PIAZZA FIUME)

Via Augusto Valenziani 19
www.chinappi.it

Family-run, fresh seafood on an ever-changing and modern menu.

PROPAGANDA (COLOSSEUM)

Via Claudia 15
www.caffepropaganda.it

Sleek modern interiors, delicious cocktails and a great menu right by the Colosseum.

FINE DINING

LA PERGOLA (MONTE MARIO)

Via Alberto Cadlolo 101
www.romecavalieri.com/it/la-pergola-it

The only restaurant in Rome with the coveted three Michelin stars has deservedly held the mantle for over 10 years.

GLASS HOSTARIA (TRASTEVERE)

Vicolo del Cinque 58
www.glass-restaurant.it

Outstanding Michelin-star dining by Rome's only female starred chef, Cristina Bowerman.

METAMORFOSI (PARIOLI)

Via Giovanni Antonelli 30
www.metamorfosiroma.it

Inventive and creative Michelin-star dining by Colombian Roy Caceres in a minimalist setting.

IMÀGO (SPAGNA)

Piazza Trinità dei Monti 6
www.hotelhasslerroma.com/en/restaurants-bars/imago

The two Michelin-star restaurant of Francesco Apreda at the famed Hotel Hassler.

MARZAPANE (SALARIO)

Via Velletri 39
www.marzapaneroma.com

Modern and refined dining with a subtle Spanish influence.

ENOTECA LA TORRE (PRATI)

Lungotevere delle Armi 22
www.enotecalatorreroma.com

Michelin-star dining in an exquisite Art Deco villa owned by the Fendi family.

TORDOMATTO (PRATI)

Via Pietro Giannone 24
www.tordomattoroma.com

Fun and contemporary fine dining by Alessandro Baldassarre with an affordable lunch tasting menu.

DELICATESSENS & CHEESEMONGERS

ANTICA CACIARA (TRASTEVERE)

Via di San Francesco a Ripa 140
Ph 06 5812815

One of the best cheese shops in Rome, and certainly the pride of Trastevere.

ANTICA NORCINERIA IACOZZILLI (TRASTEVERE)

Via Natale del Grande 15
Ph 06 5812734

Cold cuts, cheese and more, but Piero's porchetta is the star of the show here.

VOLPETTI (TESTACCIO)

Via Marmorata 47
www.volpetti.com

Gourmet food store in Testaccio with dried and fresh goods, prized cold meats and cheese.

LA TRADIZIONE (CIPRO)

Via Cipro 8
www.latradizione.it

Long-time Cipro neighbourhood
deli and cheese store.

PASTICCERIA
& FORNO

PASTICCERIA TRASTEVERE
(TRASTEVERE)

Via Natale del Grande 49
Ph 06 5818719

Trastevere's best cake shop and
a favourite with all the locals.

PASTICCERIA REGOLI
(ESQUILINO)

Via dello Statuto 60
www.pasticceriaregoli.com

A Rome institution, the cakes never
disappoint at this Esquilino outlet.

PASTICCERIA BARBERINI
(TESTACCIO)

Via Marmorata 41
www.pasticceriabarberini.it

Recently renovated, Barberini
remains a popular hangout for
cakes and coffee in Testaccio.

ANTICO FORNO ROSCIOLI
(CAMPO DE' FIORI)

Via dei Chiavari 34
www.anticofornoroscioli.it

One of the best bakeries in the city,
here you'll find all the classics; the
pizza bianca is particularly special.

BISCOTTIFICIO INNOCENTI
(TRASTEVERE)

Via della Luce 21
Ph 06 5803926

Step back in time at the biscuit
house that has been in Stefania
Innocenti's family for generations.

PASTICCERIA VALZANI
(TRASTEVERE)

Via del Moro 07
www.pasticceriavalzani.it

It's as though time has stood still in
this cake and homemade chocolates
shop. The scent when you walk
in is mesmerising.

GELATO

FATAMORGANA (TRASTEVERE)

Via Roma Libera 11
www.gelateriafatamorgana.com

One of the first gelaterie that brought
gourmet flavours to the city, from
Gorgonzola and pear to rose buds
and black rice. (Various locations)

GELATERIA DEL TEATRO (CAMPO
DE' FIORI / TRASTEVERE)

Lungotevere dei Vallati 25
www.gelateriadelteatro.it

For flavours that play on sweet and
savoury, this is natural and artisanal
gelato at its best. (Various locations)

PUNTO GELATO (CENTRO)

Piazza di Sant'Eustachio 47
www.gunthergelatoitaliano.com

Gunther Rohregger moved to Rome
from north Italy for love and you taste
that in his creations that use organic
fruit sauces and alpine water.

FIOR DI LUNA (TRASTEVERE)

Via della Lungaretta 96
www.fiordiluna.com

For gelato that faithfully follows
the produce of the season, this
is a neighbourhood favourite in
Trastevere.

COFFEE

CAFFÈ SANT'EUSTACHIO
(CENTRO)

Piazza di Sant'Eustachio 82
www.santeustachioilcaffe.com

Rome's most famous coffee house
has been serving it up since 1938.
Drink your coffee standing at the bar
like the locals.

TAZZA D'ORO (PANTHEON)

Via degli Orfani 84
www.tazzadorocoffeeshop.com

Right in front of the Pantheon,
coffee with a view doesn't get much
better than this. You can buy your
roast of choice to take home as a
souvenir too!

ROSCIOLI CAFFÈ (CAMPO DE'
FIORI)

Piazza Benedetta Cairoli 16
www.rosciolicaffe.com

Coffee served at the small bar with
the cakes Roscioli is famous for to
match. There is also a small lunch
and snack area out the back.

CRAFT BEER

MA CHE SIETE VENUTI A FÀ (TRASTEVERE)

Via Benedetta 25
www.football-pub.com

The famed Trastevere hole-in-the-wall. Grab a beer and join the locals on the street.

OPEN BALADIN (CAMPO DE' FIORI)

Via degli Specchi 6
www.openbaladin.com

Baladin beer and Gabriele Bonci joined forces to serve up some of the best beer and burgers in town in the coolest of venues.

L'OSTERIA DI BIRRA DEL BORGO (PRATI)

Via Silla 26
www.osteria.birradelborgo.it

Rome's version of a gastro pub. Casual yet high-quality food by Gabriele Bonci and a variety of craft beers.

WINE BARS

DIVIN OSTILIA (COLOSSEUM)

Via Ostilia 4
Ph 06 70496526

For a tiny neighbourhood wine experience right by the Colosseum with tasty comfort food.

LITRO (MONTEVERDE)

Via Fratelli Bonnet 5
www.vinerialitro.it

All organic and natural wines (with great cocktails too) paired with cheese and *salumi* boards and a light and seasonal menu.

AL VINO AL VINO (MONTI)

Via dei Serpenti 19
Ph 06 485803

Warm hospitality, great wine and food make this a Monti neighbourhood favourite until late into the night.

AI TRE SCALINI (MONTI)

Via Panisperna 251
Ph 06 48907495

Get in early or prepare to stand with the crowd at this longtime local hotspot for wine and hearty food.

COCKTAILS

THE JERRY THOMAS PROJECT (PIAZZA NAVONA)

Vicolo Cellini 30
www.thejerrythomasproject.it

Rome's first speakeasy, its vibe and cocktails never disappoint.

PORTO FLUVIALE (OSTIENSE)

Via del Porto Fluviale 22
www.portofluviale.com

All-day dining from pizza and *aperitivo*, to a cafe menu in a contemporary New York–style setting.

FRENI E FRIZIONI (TRASTEVERE)

Via del Politeama 4
www.freniefrizioni.com

Cool vibe and really good cocktails at this Trastevere institution.

AGAVERIA LA PUNTA (TRASTEVERE)

Via di Santa Cecilia 8
www.lapuntaexpendiodeagave.com

Mexican food and super-fun cocktails.

THE GIN CORNER (CENTRO)

Via di Pallacorda 2
Ph 06 68802452

With over 100 types available, if you're a gin lover, don't miss a drink at this bar while in town.

"I would rather be first in a village than second in Rome."
— JULIUS CAESAR

INDEX

INDEX

List of recipes

ACKNOWLEDGMENTS

I Heart Rome has been a true labour of love, and one which would have not been at all possible without the amazing support and contribution of the following people.

My immediate family — the true constants in my life and my biggest fans, distance does not separate us: my parents, Anthony, Kali, Lara, Massimo and Marco. In particular, my mum and dad, Fred and Lina, for instilling in me an unyielding appreciation of my Italian heritage which continues to define me. They encouraged me to aim high from a young age and I will be forever grateful.

My sister Lara for embracing my crazy Roman world for a year, for always being selflessly supportive of my dreams and for reading every single piece of this book before it went to print, every email, spreadsheet and brainstorm. I dedicate this to her.

Tania Calcagno for her extraordinary copy advice and Fiona Graham, for helping to turn childhood memories into prose. Fulvia Martone for her inexhaustible Italian poetry, translations and for believing in me and my crazy dreams (and for telling me years ago that I would one day write a book).

To Kate Zagorski and Angelo Preziosi (and Emilia!). There isn't enough gin in the world to thank you for your advice, assistance with recipe translations, recipes, cooking and sense of humour. Toni Brancatisano, my fellow Australian in Rome, for your baking and cooking prowess, recipes, testing and helping out in the studio (and listening to my daily rambles).

Alice Kiandra Adams for your amazing food styling, guidance, outstanding food and recipe development knowledge and sense of calm which grounded me throughout. Thank you also to your studio team, the bright Elisabetta Busini and pasta-making queen, Carla Tomasi. Marianna Martone for your love and for being my studio and on-location assistant.

To my ridiculously talented photographers Andrea Federici and Giorgia Nofrini, who managed to somehow magically capture the Rome in my heart through a camera lens.

To my friends in Rome for being my family and support system away from Australia and to all of the shopkeepers, restaurant owners and people of Rome who each hold a special place in my heart. Thank you for your cherished recipes or for allowing me to share your story: Antico Forno Roscioli & Restaurant; Secondo Tradizione; Chinappi; Alba Esteve Ruiz of Marzapane; Da Enzo al 29; Osteria der Belli; Pizzeria Da Ivo; Enoteca la Torre; Stefania Innocenti and Manuela del Gobbo of Biscottificio Innocenti; Vittorio and the team at Fatamorgana Trastevere; Signor Roberto and Signora Anna of Antica Caciara; Marco Lori; I Supplì; Paolo Tocchio; the team at The Jerry Thomas Project; Stefano Callegari; Agostino and the entire team at Trapizzino; Laura Ravaioli; Gina Tringali; and cheese goddess Eleonora Baldwin. And my wonderful friends who shared their recipes and hearts with me: Fernanda Menozzi, Viviana Gori, Maurizio Misso and Eleonora Chiari.

Much gratitude to Beatrice Mencattini and Beatrice Tarizzo of Aromi Creativi; Chiara di Fonzo, Flavia Campailla and Paolo Dianini and the entire bar team at Hotel de Russie; Barbara Manto, Angelo Severini and the staff at Rome Cavalieri, Waldorf Astoria Hotel. Thanks also to special friends and colleagues Sabrina Tocchio, Ramona Maeola, Carla Andronaco, Belinda Bortolan, Annie Ojile, Robyn Woodman, Kenny Dunn, Franca Smarrelli and Paola Bacchia. And heartfelt thanks to chef Cristina Bowerman for your generosity, kindness and encouragement.

Massive love to all my recipe testers: Lina Pasquale, Lara Pasquale, Kali Pasquale, Angela Pasquale, Lisa Pasquale, Melissa Castiglia, Tania Calcagno, Anna Calcagno, Danielle Guarnaccia, Paula Mannello-Mammoliti, Lucia Mannello, Maria Caratozzolo, Connie Caratozzolo, Diana Tandora, Laura Franzo, Justine Marchitto, Fernando Garcia, Maria Colosimo, Valerie Pancari, Patricia De Fazio, Lora Caruana, Anita Bekavac, Christine Kelso and Meg Kolac.

Thank you to Paul McNally of Smith Street Books for believing in, and taking a risk with me. Big thanks to his project and editing team Aisling Coughlan and Katri Hilden and to designer Murray Batten for turning my Roman world into gorgeous fonts and colours.

To my HeartRome followers on the blog and across social media, for your kinds words of encouragement from the very beginning and throughout this entire journey. This book is as much yours as it is mine.

ABOUT THE AUTHOR

Born to Italian parents, in Melbourne Australia, Maria always knew Rome was her destiny.

Graduating with a double degree in Arts (political science and history) and Public Policy and Management from the University of Melbourne in 2001, she began her career as an Adviser for the State Government of Victoria. Her passion for writing and communication eventually led her into the corporate world of PR and events and by the age of 30 she had established her own company.

With over 15 years of experience working across the public, private and community sector, she is an expert PR, events and social media strategist, having serviced international clients in Australia and across Europe, including MasterCard, Italy's top rated food tour company, Eating Europe Tours and international tourism boards.

Based in Rome since 2011, she is now an award-winning food and travel writer and journalist and contributes regularly to USA Today, Condé Nast, Fodor's, CNN and The Telegraph. She has interviewed some of the world's greatest chefs and spent thousands of hours talking and learning from passionate and dedicated food lovers the globe over.

An unabashed romantic (Rome being her one true love) she created the lifestyle blog HeartRome in 2011. The blog has readers in over 100 countries, a 30,000 strong social media following and has been featured in BBC Travel and Vogue among others. Maria has built a career by linking her skills and experience with her true passion for new experiences and a love of the history and culture of food. Not only has she followed this journey from Melbourne to Rome, but around the world from Oslo to Paris, New York to Hong Kong and Dubai to St Petersburg.

In one true story, she flew across Europe to dine amongst a table of strangers because she was offered a last-minute seat at a world renowned Michelin star restaurant. Her insatiable desire to discover and explore the culinary world makes her equally excited about new openings as the honouring of old traditions.

In Rome, you'll find her walking the streets of Trastevere, checking out the latest bar for an *aperitivo* or dining at a local *trattoria* with friends.

I Heart Rome is Maria's first book.

"While stands the Coliseum, Rome shall stand; When falls the Coliseum, Rome shall fall; And when Rome falls—the world."
— LORD BYRON

Smith Street Books

Published in 2017 by Smith Street Books
Melbourne | Australia
smithstreetbooks.com

ISBN: 978-19254-1855-2

The moral right of the author has been asserted.
CIP data is available from the National Library of Australia.

Publisher: Paul McNally
Project Manager: Aisling Coughlan
Editor: Katri Hilden
Designer: Murray Batten
Food photography: Giorgia Nofrini & Andrea Federici
Location & profile photography: Andrea Federici
Food styling: Alice Kiandra Adams
Food preparation: Alice Kiandra Adams, Angelo Preziosi, Toni Brancatisano
    with assistance from Carla Tomasi, Elisabetta Busini
Translations support: Kate Zagorski

Printed & bound in China by C&C Offset Printing Co., Ltd.

Book 43
10 9 8 7 6 5 4 3 2 1